Whispers of Marriage

from

EDEN
DEVOTIONAL WORKBOOK

By Rachelle M Smith

Whispers of Marriage from EDEN -
DEVOTIONAL WORKBOOK
Copyright © 2025 by Rachelle M Smith
ISBN: 9781763784956
Self-publishing, Printed in Australia.

All rights reserved solely by the author. The author guarantees all contents are original and do not infringe upon the legal rights of any other persons or work. No portion of this book may be reproduced in any form or by any means - electronic, mechanical, photocopy, recording, scanning, or other - except for brief quotations in personal use, without prior permission from the author/publisher.

Unless otherwise indicated, Scriptures are taken from THE HOLY BIBLE NEW INTERNATIONAL VERSION. Copyright © 1973, 1978, 1984 by International Bible Society; Zondervan; Grand Rapids, Michigan 49530, USA.

Scriptures noted NKJV, Nelson's Study Bible. Copyright © 1979, 1980, 1982, 1997; Thomas Nelson, Inc. United States of America.

Scriptures noted NCV, Max Lucado; The Devotional Bible (Experiencing the heart of Jesus), Copyright © 1987, 1988, 1991, 2003, by Word publishing, a didion of Thomas Nelson, Inc. All rights reserved.

Scripture noted ESV, English Standard Version, Copyright © 2001, 2007, 2011, 2016, Crossway Bibles, Publishing ministry of Good News Bibles Publishers.

Scriptures noted AMPC, Amplified Bible, Classic Edition, Holy Bible app.

Scriptures notes CEV, Contemporary English Version, Copyright © American Bible Society, Youversion App.

Version 4.4.2

MORRISVILLE NORTH CAROLINA UNITED STATES FRANCE THE UNITED KINGDOM AUSTRALIA CANADA INDIA

www.lulu.com

Copyright © 2024 Lulu Press, Inc. All rights reserved.

Self-Publishing, Since 2002

All printing, editing, page format, and layout created by RACHELLE M SMITH using *Lulu* Publishing.

http://www.canva.com

All front cover images, layout, style and font designs created by RACHELLE M SMITH using *Canva*.

Acknowledgment

To my husband and best friend, thank you for always believing and encouraging me.

I wrote *'Whispers of Marriage from EDEN'* then added the *'Devotional Workbook'* for singles/couples to study in the knowledge and relationship of God.

To my extended family and friends, thank you for believing in me. Thank you for standing with us as a couple. Thank you for your words of encouragement to go further with God. I couldn't have asked God for more loyal and true friends to journey with me during my writings.

May this *Devotional Workbook* bring fruitful discussions, further insight, knowledge, growth and empower your relationship with roots grounded deeper in Gods word and everlasting love.

About This Interactive Book

This *Devotional Workbook* may be read cover to cover, similar to other books. However, I encourage you to read and explore the optional elements for a more enriched personalised experience. There are ten chapters. Each chapter is sectioned into five daily devotions with corresponding questions at the end. You have the choice of working through each chapter by yourself as a couple or as a group. You can choose to complete one devotion and questions per day or you can adapt these elements to your own preference.

I suggest those participating in this study read the corresponding chapters in *'Whispers of Marriage from Eden'* book first, to better understand the background and devotions for each chapter. If you are reading this book as part of a ministry series study, I recommend that you offer the appropriate qualified counselling support services required throughout the topics and questions that may open private or sensitive discussions throughout this book.

There is one teaching session for each chapter in this book. Discussion questions are located after each, daily devotion. This *Devotional Workbook* is designed for singles/couples to work through together or in a supported group environment.

Who is this book for?

This is a simple and unique Devotional Workbook to not only help couples discuss marital life, but to heal, move forward and to identify areas that require attention, as well as being aware of the healthy and unhealthy signs of a relationship. If you are already marriage or want to gain a better understanding of marriage. Maybe you need help or support with your journey. Because, we are living in days where there is not much knowledge or wisdom being passed on. There is so much divorce and distortion, many are afraid to share their stories. What path you have once walked need not to define your correct path God is leading you towards.

Then, there are those who feel trapped with deep topics. I don't want you to close the book on marriage but rather I want to help you turn each page. There are also countless friends and family members who believed their love stories would never end, only to discover the pages that reveal deep topics of discussion are abruptly torn from their lives by divorce or the loss of a spouse. If only Disney movies had it right. Happily ever after from the moment the prince and princess ride off into the sunset. The truth is that riding into the sunset is only the beginning. Your happy ever after isn't over!

This is not a comprehensive book where is unpacks every dimension of marriage. Volumes could still be written on Marriage. I wanted to explore the 'life' that goes into a marriage. I don't have all the answers. I decided to pen my story and knowledge to offer hope to those who need it most.

We all make mistakes, yet Jesus still thinks marriage is a story worth sharing. It is His framework for how He loves each of us. I pray these pages stir your faith, hope and love in both the single and married, both the young as well as those experienced along the years.

I dare you to explore your love again!

Table of Contents

Chapter 1. The Tree of Life
- Your love story
- Adam and Eve
- I have a choice
- Purpose for marriage

Chapter 2. Once upon a marriage…
- Jacob and Rachel
- Marriage, a sacred union
- Iron sharpens iron
- Contract Vs. Covenant

Chapter 3. Old Baggage
- Handling your baggage
- Excess Baggage
- Just in Case
- Ditch excess baggage

Chapter 4. With this Ring
- The wedding ring
- Love is a sacrifice
- Relationship with God
- The vow of preparation

Chapter 5. A Nautical View
- Equally Yoked
- Christs Coordinates
- Below the water level
- Hope after the storm

CHAPTER 6. TOP SECRET
- HONOUR YOUR WIFE
- SUPPORT YOUR HUSBAND
- HEAD SERVANT
- ROLES FOR HUSBAND AND WIFE

CHAPTER 7. IN2MACY
- FIVE STAGES OF INTIMACY
- MARRIAGE VS. DISABILITY
- PORNOGRAPHY VS. INTIMACY
- INTIMACY WITH GOD

CHAPTER 8. START WITH THE END IN MIND
- HAVING FUN IN YOUR MARRIAGE
- THE BRIDE OF CHRIST
- RUNNING THE RACE
- KEYS TO A HAPPY MARRIAGE

CHAPTER 9. HONEY…WE NEED TO TALK!
- MONEY TALKS
- FAMILY COMMUNICATION
- RAISING TOMORROWS BRIDE AND GROOM
- TALKING VS. LISTENING

CHAPTER 10. SOMETHING OLD, SOMETHING NEW
- LETTING GO OF THE OLD
- A BEAUTIFUL CRY
- KNOWN AND LOVED
- A UNITED MARRIAGE

Introduction

The phrase 'Pass (on) the baton' is an action we see in athletic sports, however to use this phrase in a marriage context refers to our responsibility to hand over knowledge, wisdom and experience. After writing *'Whispers of Marriage from Eden'* which later won two gold seal awards, I felt the topics and questions throughout the chapters required a *'Devotional Workbook'* to help equip couples; to enrich their relationship.

Somewhere along the way generations have dropped the *'baton'*, and real love stories within long lasting marriages have become few and far between. Reflecting on Biblical values, what worked for our ancestors and the generation who walked in marriage before us, is the same sentimental journey we can instill not only into our own lives, by passing on this baton of marital knowledge to the next generation.

A marriage simply consists of three things; Friendship, Commitment, and Gods Covenant, everything else is *life*. Further, a happy marriage is built on three things too; memories of togetherness, forgiveness of mistakes, and the promise to never give up on each other. It's how you respond to the warning signs and walk through life together that will determine your healthy or unhealthy loving marital destiny.

Love comes from God, of course. But how do you know that you have the real thing? Look at how love behaves. If others don't easily annoy you, if you can rejoice while others are winning and you aren't, if you don't feel the need to toot your own horn, and if its easy to show others that you care, you have the real thing.

If none of this comes easy, don't despair. A fresh dose of God's loving presence is always available. You only need to ask. As you do, you'll find a love that stands up to tough times and obstinate people and keeps on loving with creative acts of compassion and care.

As my husband and I journey with God, we never forget that our marriage is our story, it's just that: it is ours. Our life and marriage holds a collection of joys, victories and challenges, yet, like the tree of life, the roots of our relationship are grounded in God. God made our marriage…not us! It's His Spirit that inhabits every detail of your marriage. Not only did God create your marriage, He is personally involved in your process as two human beings become one.

Chapter One
The Tree of Life

'The LORD God made all kinds of trees grow out of the ground - trees that were pleasing to the eye and good for food. In the middle of the garden were the tree of life and the tree of the knowledge of good and evil'.

- Genesis 2:9

Devotion Day 1. The Tree of Life

In order to begin this study guide we need to take a look back to where the first relationship began. Back to where we can only imagine the magnificence of trees which grew in such extraordinary environments. The Garden of Eden. A beautiful garden wrapped around two trees. This was no ordinary day, nor were these ordinary trees, in fact this was the first wedding day. Each tree was a flawless symbol of life rooted in rich soil, awakened by cascading water, and nourished by radiant-yet tempered-sunshine. Whilst there were many trees in the garden, scripture only mentions two: the tree of life and the tree of knowledge of good and evil. Both trees enjoyed the same immaculate and unpolluted conditions - a state of existence that this fallen world could never replicate. Yet only one tree delivered life, the other death.

Every story of marriage has an origin with these two trees of Eden. In many ways, our marriages in the world today can be likened to these two trees. We each have a <u>choice</u> to marry into a healthy relationship and yet, often we fall into temptation and choose the wrong relationship (wrong tree), and end up in a friendship with someone, or committed relationship that is leading to a marriage which reeks toxins of unhealthy love. Marriages grow in different seasons whilst growing and doing their best when making the right choices and a maturing root system.

The image of this books cover provides a glimpse into the life of a tree. What we see is a circle, a round ring. When you cut a tree trunk horizontally you can see a lot of round rings which actually tells the story of the tree's life. Its the fingerprint of its growth and journey.

Think back to your school days. Many of us learnt the science of gardening or were taught by our parents how to plant a tree. Today, many of us including our younger children are being taught the study of plants by the famous English biologist David Attenborough.

The study of woody plants can be done by anyone. You can determine the age of the tree by simply counting the rings. Whilst we are far from having the exuberant mind of David Attenboroughs dendrology studies.

We can be reassured with a trees exact age by expert tree lovers who provide us with intimate details of a tree's life by simply observing the cross section.

To the trained eye, each ring is a story. The varying band of rings reveal the width which can tell if the tree has experienced a mild or extremely harsh winter, revealing patterns of drought or abundant rain.

A closer inspection can indicate incidents of injury, attacks of pests and scars from forrest fires. Each ring is a year of seasons, and similar to our wedding ring the circular formation is somewhat of fashion and unique in nature.

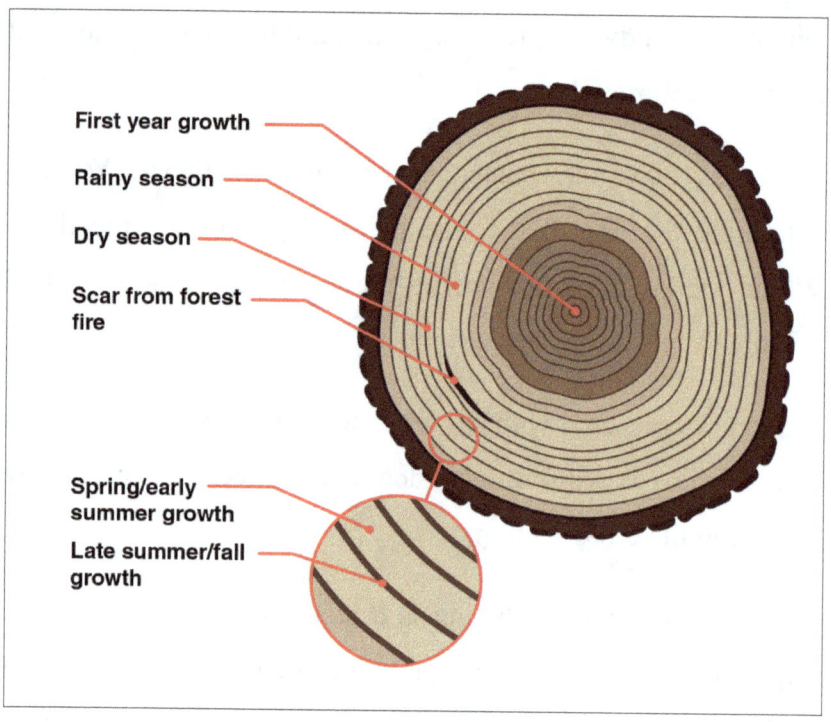

Each year of your marriage can be likened to the path of a tree ring - circular in fashion and unique in nature. Anniversaries mark the end of one year and the beginning of the next. The annual date is highlighted by the months, weeks, and days that fill the calendar year all add up to your collection of joys, pain, work, and even surprises.

Day 1 Devotional Questions
The Tree of Life

'There is a time for everything, and a season for every activity under heavens'.

- Ecclesiastes 3:1 NIV

Summer, Autumn, Winter and Spring, are seasons which bring its own joys and challenges.

For example; **Summer.** Just like our weather outside, things are hot in summer and everything appears tropical and beautiful. That's what it's like in a relationship when it's first starting out. You fall deeply in love with your spouse and everything is perfect. They can do no wrong and all we see is the good. Remember those days? This is summer.

Then there's **Autumn**. Things start to cool down. The leaves start falling off the trees. Likewise in marriage. The honeymoon period is starting to fade away. Maybe they're not meeting your needs. Maybe you're starting to have some resentment creep in because you're not resolving conflicts well.

When it turns to **Winter**, things become frosty. Outside looks lifeless and dreary. Winter often brings a lack of sunlight and activity. This is a very sad time and likewise in marriage. Hurt, anger, disappointment, loneliness, rejection, and sometimes hopelessness are some of the emotions that couples experience when their marriage in this season of *winter* often ending in separation or divorce.

Spring is when the warmth starts to come back. The trees start to bloom again, flowers bloom, and wonderful fragrances are in the air. Likewise in your marriage, when you go through *spring*, the warmth and the love feelings start coming back. Your needs start to be met more. Just like the trees in the garden of Eden, it's vital that you know all marriages go through the four seasons of marriage so that when they arrive you're prepared. What season are you in now? Are you in Summer? Are you in Autumn? Or, are you in Winter or Spring?

The Tree of Life model is about thriving, not just surviving, and helping others do the same. It addresses brokenness and trauma as part of one's history, a place to find healing.

What would you say is one of your best seasons you have shared with your spouse? Briefly describe it and share why it is so memorable to you.

_____
_____
_____
_____

How would you describe the most challenging storms you have experienced as a marital couple? Who did you turn to? How did you make it through? What did God teach you?

_____
_____
_____
_____

Take a moment. What season would you say your marriage is currently in? How could you enjoy this season more?

_____
_____
_____
_____

Over the years your unique 'blueprint' of building blocks has shaped your marriage and life becomes clearer. Take time now to be still and appreciate it. What has made your marriage so special? Consider the gifts, personalities, desires, goals, and experiences.

_____
_____
_____
_____
_____
_____
_____
_____
_____
_____

Pause and Pray

'Lord, You made the seasons from the very beginning. The change of seasons has always been a part of Your promise - that they will never cease. We know when seasons in our own lives come and go, it is for Your good. Bless us through every season of our marriage'.

In Jesus Name - Amen

DEVOTION DAY 2. YOUR LOVE STORY

As you begin this study with me, remember that your story (or future story) is just that: *it belongs to you.* How sad it would be to get to the end of your life as an old person and realise, I didn't love others the way I should. It would then be too late. This is a big topic, but nevertheless, an important one. Sometimes people say, What's the point of trying to love others? It only gets thrown back in my face. They mean they have had unfortunate experiences when their gesture of love has been misunderstood or rejected, and they don't want to get hurt again. However, this is life, you will get hurt sometime in this life, and your love to others may not be properly understood or appreciated. It is God who says, '*Just as I have loved you, so you should love one another*'. It's a commandment from God Himself, and we need to take that seriously.

A happy marriage is built on three things, memories of togetherness, forgiveness of mistakes, and the promise to never give up on each other. It's how you respond to the warning signs and walk through life together that will determine your unhealthy or healthy loving marital destiny. As my husband and I journey with God, we never forget that our marriage is our story, it's just that: it is ours. Our life and marriage holds a collection of joys, victories and challenges, yet, like the tree of life the roots of our relationship are grounded in God. God made our marriage…not us! It's His Spirit that inhabits every detail of your marriage. Not only did God create your marriage, He is personally involved in your process as two human beings become one. Every life and marriage holds a collection of joys, victories and challenges. For too long, much of the church has prescribed a generic approach to solve problems that threaten, our marriages. We have been taught 'Wives, submit, and Husbands love'. Although there is substance and truth to this scripture, honestly, there is no 'one-size fits all' advice which fits all marriages. Because each marriage is made from God and comes with its own unique blueprint.

Let's look at this another way.

The blueprints for every home requires a solid foundation which also supports the walls and roof. However, the builders have the creative ability and freedom to design according to the specific needs and hearts desires of its occupants. It's the same with our marriages. We have been given a choice to design our marriage that will best suit us, each having its own domain that offers freedom that varies with the seasons of life. Constructing a marriage and I believe this blueprint of marriage bliss is something to be hungry for. You wouldn't dream of building a home without any blueprints, after all without the blueprints your new home would be structurally unsound! Every beautiful home begins with a well thought out plan and design. It's only after the plan is drafted that the builders can construct the house, doing so with hard work, the correct tools, and right materials. Blueprints are also essential for determining the cost of construction.

So it is with your marriage. We are granted the creative license to design according to the specific needs and desires of its inhabitants. Each domain should appear different and offer the freedom to vary with the seasons of life. In our marriage we have transferred from seasons of working full time, parenting full time, to now being at home full time together everyday. This means we need to find ways to enjoy each others company more the more we are apart.

After all absence makes the heart grow fonder. Such change in our marriage is as natural as the changing seasons. All of this is natural and to be expected. There are worldly, eternal truths and values that will fast forward your marriage into everything God has created it to be. God Himself wants each united couple to be built with love, respect, joy, submission, provision, faithfulness, nature, intimacy and above all, legacy. Whatever way you build these blocks in your life will reflect the uniqueness of your personalities and the season of your marriage. God reveals the major principals but leaves room for your expression in the particulars.

I want to make it clear from the start that we do not believe all couples fit into a generic marriage mould. Todays statistics show that not all spouses work outside the home. Since 2020, the lockdown of Covid brought opportunities for many to work in the safety of their own home. We are living in times of equal jobs and equal pay rights. Yet, the ability to produce more income does not mean you submit differently or view your husband less of a leader. It simply means you are both contributing to the household income. This is exactly what our Grandparents did. Our marriage reflects this, we both work in different areas of ministry. Sometimes we work together, sometimes we work apart, yet the goal of our marriage and our underlying values do not hinder. Our husband and wife relationship roles hold no competitive mindset with our ability to produce income. In the garden of Eden, God told both Adam and Eve to be fruitful and multiply. The woman in

Proverbs 31 reads of an amazing household manager and entrepreneur, this woman was strong. If this is what sounds right for your marriage, then follow this design. Or one of you may want to stay at home full-time raising the children. There is nothing wrong with either of these approaches. It appears that what works well for others will work well for you. Yet, we are in unique days that will challenge rising costs on every front. I want your marriage to be strong. This means you must have the freedom to built your marriage of your dreams, not the marriage of someone else's dream.

Building a life together, like building a house, takes wisdom. Without the right foundation, even a small storm can topple a large structure. Without good workmanship, repairs are soon needed and problems multiply.

No matter what you try and accomplish in life together, choosing to invite God into the process, to give Him the leadership role, means the difference between success and failure. Opposing the purpose of God, would be like sweeping a driveway in the middle of a storm. You would't be able to clear the path. Defining to God's will and wisdom in all you do, however, allows Him to establish the work of our hands. God grants success that lasts forever.

The God who made you, redeemed you, and loves you has already given you a glorious blueprint for your marriage. God's blueprint stands in stark contrast to the world's plan. The world counsels us to fight for our own rights or leave our spouse if our needs are not being met. But God's plan is different and far more beautiful. It involves submitting to one another out of reverence for Christ, confronting the sin in our own hearts before confronting it in each other, and forgiving our spouse, as often as it takes. This is God's countercultural plan for marriage, designed to make our marriages flourish.

I encourage you to take a moment to seek God's Holy Spirit, who is our friend and spirit of truth. Ask God to reveal how His eternal truths can transform your marriage into a phenomenal union - the one He designed just for you, where it all started in the Garden of Eden.

'Give in to God, come to terms with Him and everything will turn out just fine. Let Him tell you what to do'.

- Job 22:21 MSG

Day 2 Devotional Questions

Your Love Story

GOD, not you, made marriage, His Spirit inhibits even the smallest details of marriage

- Malachi 2:15 (MSG)

God made marriage, and it is very important to Him - so important in fact He desires to be intimately involved in every aspect of your relationship. His word says; You're cheating on God. If all you want is your own way, flirting with the world every chance you get, you end up enemies of God and his way. And do you suppose God doesn't care?

The proverb has it that 'he's a fiercely jealous lover'. And what he gives in love is far better than anything else you'll find. It's common knowledge that 'God opposes the proud; but shows favour to the humble'. (James 4:5 NIV)

Stop and think. Have you invited the Holy Spirit into every area of your marriage. If you have only invited Him into parts of your marriage, how is life different when you forget to involve Him?

_____
_____
_____
_____
_____

We all have the privilege of talking to God anytime, anywhere about anything. What are your challenges? Are you struggling with fear? Financial challenges? Are you having difficulty communicating? Why not take these challenges to God in prayer? Take time and carefully read the following scriptures and write down what the Holy Spirit reveals.

1. Philippians 4:6-7 2. 1 Peter 5:7
3. Matthew 6:25-34

_____
_____
_____
_____

4. Matthew 7:7-11   5. John 14:13-14   6. 1 John 5:14-15

_____
_____
_____
_____
_____

God does't want your marriage to be a battle field or war zone. He desires it to be your Eden, a place of pleasure and delight. What would you like God to change in your marriage? After you answer, Spend time with God, ask Him 'What is my part in seeing this happen? What needs to change in me'?

_____
_____
_____
_____
_____
_____
_____
_____
_____

You may be encouraged with the assurance of your own love story of marriage that God will never leave you nor forsake you. Or perhaps you are gladdened by the pledge that when God is your delight, He will give you the desires of your heart. Yet, sometimes the promise is more personal. Whatever the promise is, as you both journey through life, God will never forget or break His word. He will see it done in your life. Just like a proposal, God's answer is Yes and amen!

What has God promised you individually and as a couple?

_____
_____
_____
_____
_____

Pause and Pray

'LORD BLESS OUR MARRIAGE. HELP US REMEMBER WITH GRATITUDE THE LOVE STORY YOU'RE WRITING IN OUR LIVES. LET US NOT TAKE YOUR PROMISES FOR GRANTED.
IN JESUS NAME - AMEN

Devotion Day 3. Adam and Eve

Now, no shrub had yet appeared on the earth and no plant had yet sprung up, for the Lord God had not sent rain on the earth and there was no one to work the ground. Streams came up from the earth and watered the whole surface of the ground. Then the Lord God formed a man from the dust of the ground and breathed into his nostrils the breath of life, and the man became a living being.

Now the Lord God had planted a garden in the east, in Eden; and there he put the man he had formed. The Lord God made all kinds of trees grow out of the ground—trees that were pleasing to the eye and good for food. In the middle of the garden were the tree of life and the tree of the knowledge of good and evil.

A river watering the garden flowed from Eden; from there it was separated into four headwaters. The name of the first is the Pishon; it winds through the entire land of Havilah, where there is gold. (The gold of that land is good; aromatic resin and onyx are also there.) The name of the second river is the Gihon; it winds through the entire land of Cush. The name of the third river is the Tigris; it runs along the east side of Ashur. And the fourth river is the Euphrates.

Genesis 2:17 reads, The Lord God took the man and put him in the Garden of Eden to work it and take care of it. And the Lord God commanded the man, *'You are free to eat from any tree in the garden; but you must not eat from the tree of the knowledge of good and evil, for when you eat from it you will certainly die'.* The Lord God said, *'It is not good for the man to be alone. I will make a helper suitable for him'. Now the Lord God had formed out of the ground all the wild animals and all the birds in the sky. He brought them to the man to see what he would name them; and whatever the man called each living creature, that was its name. So the man gave names to all the livestock, the birds in the sky and all the wild animals. But for Adam no suitable helper was found. So the Lord God caused the man to fall into a deep sleep; and while he was sleeping, he took one of the man's ribs and then closed up the place with flesh. Then the Lord God made a woman from the rib he had taken out of the man, and he brought her to the man'.*

- Genesis 2:22.

The man said, *'This is now bone of my bones and flesh of my flesh; she shall be called 'woman' for she was taken out of man.* That is why a man leaves his father and mother and is united to his wife, and they become 'one flesh'. The tree of life! It sounds poetic, almost a romantic name for a tree. It ignites the imagination thus, producing wonderful images of growth, life, as well as branching off a bright future and good times. Most of us familiar with the term know that the tree of life is mentioned in the Bible in the early chapters of the book of Genesis. We associate it with Adam the man and Eve the woman, as well as their sin that separated them from God. Today, theologians refer to this deep hidden romance which flourished and grew is known as *'the first wedding'*.

Author Frank Viola shares his thoughts from his book 'Eternity to Here', he writes:

> *'In Genesis 1 and 2, the Bible opens up with a woman and a man. In Revelation 21 and 22, the Bible closes with a woman and a man. The Bible opens up with a wedding, and it ends with a wedding. It opens with a marriage, and it ends with a marriage. It opens with a boy and a girl, and it ends with a boy and a girl. Your Bible is essentially a love story'.*

So, now we have this picture of a man named Adam who was the only human on earth and yet to understand this man and scripture in full, you can start to feel that this one man...this one man on earth felt a need within himself that no other creature shared. Something inside of him desperately longed for freedom and release. This yearning was 'passion'. God himself put within Adams beating chest an intense all-consuming passion as well as an overwhelming sense of love, however, up until this point, Adam was 'alone'.

So, as we understand the story, Adam could not pour out his passion and love upon a life form which was different from his own. He desired a companion, someone who would compliment him, a creature like himself who would be the receiver of his passion and love. Let's fast forward to the seventh day recalling that Gods creation is finished, we are now nearing the eighth day, thus being the first day of the week. The picture of Adams world is getting bigger. It was evening. And God does something phenomenal, He puts Adam into a deep sleep. I will show you a mystery; There was a woman hidden inside of Adam. Note, creation has finished, so this woman was not part of the first creation. She appears on the eighth day, surprisingly this woman is in fact a new creation.

Adam and Eve were made in the image of God, but not equal to Him. The *image* of something speaks of a reflection, not a representation in its entirety. The deceived and disobedient couple were banished from the garden. They would never again have access to the living fruit found on the tree of life. Without this living fruit, Adam and Eve were doomed to mortality. They died, and their garden is long gone. Yet, in many ways they live, because we are their offspring. Men and woman no longer have individual immortality on earth, but marriage is the way of life to continue through reproduction.

The good news throughout this message is that the cross of Christ is now our ultimate tree of life. It restores everything that was lost in the garden. A godly marriage can serve as a life-flourishing tree. It provided the necessary structure for both legacy as well as intimacy. This is why it's so crucial to God that we honour marriage, guard the spirit and love each other with all of our very being.

It doesn't take a relationship expert to tell us something significant has been lost in translation between the Garden and now. Many marriages are the opposite of a life flourishing tree. Divorce, adultery, addictions, disappointments, unhealthy relationships, offences of abuse cripple our marriage and homes. Because of this lack in love, many do not understand the power and purpose of marriages or why they should get married. Others who are married are just trying to survive the cross fire, holding on to what ever flame of love they can. To them, marriage isn't a safe place. It's now a war zone.

There maybe times when everything in your circumstances will tell you that God has forgotten you, that He doesn't care. Any marriage that walks with God needs to be prepared for moments such as these. This is when you press forward. God's love never fails. The reward is on the other side, after the storm a rainbow appears. You can endure the test and climb marriage together with faith. Our relationship with God, broken by sin, can be reconciled through Jesus Christ. Our sinful nature may have been born in the Garden of Eden, but it is put to death on the cross. We do not have to be separated from God. The indwelling of His Spirit means that we can once again talk with Him, walk with Him, and experience His majesty every hour of the day.

Can you think of a time your sin affected other people?

Day 3 Devotional Questions
Adam and Eve

Sometimes I wonder how the story would have turned out if you or I had been the one in the garden instead of Adam and Eve. In our own mindset we could have tried to resist the temptation to eat from the forbidden tree. However, the truth is, Adam and Eve used their free will to turn against God. I am guilty of rebelling against Him too. We all are.

I also wonder if Adam and Eve understood the full impact of their consequences. One act of disobedience affected all of creation, the history of the entire world, especially mankind. Sin created a wall between them and God. They had never been separated from God so how could they know or imagine what it would be like if He wasn't there? What would it be like not to talk to Him, walk with Him, and experience His majesty every hour of the day not just for them but for everyone? Hard work, painful childbirth, and physical death were part of God's consequences. Yet, those were nothing compared to the absence of God.

In the same way, we don't always understand the full weight of our choices either. We can't see the big picture, or the ripple effect of our choices. Often we don't know if or how it will affect other people. The personal consequences are more obvious. Sin separates us from God as much today as it did back in the garden of Eden. When we don't allow the Holy Spirit to convict us and shamefully try to hide our sins from God, as if that's possible, it separates us even further. Read scripture Genesis 2:7, discuss and answer the following:

In what way was man different to the other living creatures? What was his purpose?

_____
_____
_____
_____

Why was Eve created? What was her purpose?

_____
_____
_____
_____

What was the nature of Adam and Eve's relationship?

___

What was their relationship with God and his creation?

___

Read Genesis 3:1-5. What commandment did God give Adam? What did He say the consequences would be of breaking this rule?

___

How did the serpent undermine God's authority? Was the serpent lying?

___

Read Genesis 3:1-19. What was it about the forbidden fruit that tempted Eve? What did Adam do?

_____
_____
_____
_____
_____

How did Adam and Eve try to hide or excuse their shame?

_____
_____
_____
_____
_____

PAUSE AND PRAY

'LORD, BLESS OUR MARRIAGE, WE THANK YOU FOR THIS DAY AND FOR OUR LIFE. WE THANK YOU THAT YOU ARE OUR GOD, OUR CREATOR, AND OUR SAVIOUR'.

IN JESUS NAME - AMEN

Devotion Day 4. I have a Choice

The Bible is full of life, families, drama, births, deaths, love stories, family crises, sickness, war, lies, betrayal, forgiveness, hope, loneliness, trust, barrenness, passion, wisdom, strength, and most of all love. So, why then, did God put the tree of knowledge of good *and* evil in the Garden of Eden? It appears the trees were planted in order to give both Adam and Eve a <u>choice</u> to either obey God or disobey God. Adam and Eve were free to do anything they wanted to, except eat from the tree of knowledge of good and evil. Genesis 2:16-17 reads *"And the LORD God commanded the man, You are free to eat from any tree in the garden; but you must not eat from the tree of the knowledge of good and evil, for when you eat of it you will surely die"*. Their <u>choice</u> in disobeying God brought corruption into their lives or let's say, their relationship and marriage and into the world. Eating the fruit, was an act of disobedience against God. God did not want Adam and Eve to sin. God knew ahead of time what the results of sin would be.

Because of what Jesus did for us on the cross, you are free, you are free to choose…

I am free to choose love. Today I will love God and what God loves.

I am free to choose joy. I will invite God into my marital walk and into every circumstance. I will refuse to see people as anything less than human beings, created by God. I will refuse to see any problem as anything less than an opportunity to see God.

I choose peace. I will live forgiven. I will forgive so that I may live.

I choose patience. I will overlook the inconveniences of the world. Instead of cursing the one who takes my place, I'll invite Him to do so. Rather than complain that the wait is too long, I will thank God for a moment to pray. Instead of clenching my fist at new assignments, I will face them with joy and courage.

I am free to choose kindness. I will be kind to the poor, for they are alone. Kind to the rich, for they are afraid. And kind to the unkind, for such is how God has treated me.

I am free to choose goodness. I will go without a dollar before I take a dishonest one. I will be overlooked before I will boast. I will confess before I will accuse. I choose goodness.

I am free to choose faithfulness. Today I will keep my promises. My debtors will not regret their trust. My associates will not question my word. My wife will not question my love. My children will never fear that their father will not come home.

I am free to choose gentleness. Nothing is won by force. I choose to be gentle. If I raise my voice, may it be only in praise. If I clench my fist, may it be only in prayer. If I make a demand, may it be only of myself.

I am free to choose self-control. I am a spiritual being. After this body is dead, my spirit will soar. I refuse to let what will rot, rule the eternal. I choose self-control. I will be drunk only by joy. I will be impassioned only by my faith. I will be influenced only by God. I will be taught only by Christ. I choose self-control.

Love, joy, peace, patience, kindness, goodness, faithful-ness, gentleness, and self-control. To these I commit my day. If I succeed, I will give thanks. If I fail, I will seek God's grace. And then, when this day is done, I will place my head on my pillow and rest.

'For you were called to freedom, brothers. Only do not use your freedom as an opportunity for the flesh, but through love serve one another. For the whole law is fulfilled in one word: 'You shall love your neighbour as yourself'.

- Galatians 5:13-14

'Live as people who are free, not using your freedom as a cover-up for evil, but living as servants of God'.

- 1 Peter 2:16

As you live and navigate through this world, let us not grow weary and lose sight of the big picture. TRUE FREEDOM IS IN JESUS CHRIST ALONE! He sets us free from the bondage of this world if we confess our sins and make Him Lord and Saviour of our lives. There isn't anybody here on earth, no matter how powerful they are, that can take that away. So be encouraged by His grace, pursue Him daily, and walk in true freedom today!

Day 4 Devotional Questions
I Have a Choice

In the morning, with the rising of the sun the stillness of the dawn will be exchanged for the noise of the day. The calm of solitude will be replaced by the pounding pace of the human race. For the next twelve hours I will be exposed to the day's demands. As I wake, rise from my pillow of rest, it is now that I must make a choice. I will love God and what God loves. I choose joy. I choose peace. I will live forgiven. I choose patience. Rather than complain. I'll thank God for a moment to pray. I choose kindness, for that's how God has treated me. I choose goodness. I choose faithfulness. Today I'll keep my promises. My spouse will not question my love. I choose gentleness. If I make a demand, may it be only of myself. I choose self-control. I will be impassioned only by my faith and influenced only by God. I choose the tree of life!

Life is full of hard choices, and the bigger they are and the more options we have, the harder they get. Making choices and decisions are a part of life. Simply put, the way life unfolds, with its twists and turns, starts and stops, requires us to make choices and decisions every step of the way. Some people have been burned in the past by poor choices and decisions and are afraid to, once again, risk making a bad choice or decision. So they may do nothing hoping the change will work itself out, or go away, or that somebody else will take care of what needs to be done.

What choices or decisions are you struggling with today?

_____
_____
_____
_____
_____
_____
_____
_____
_____
_____
_____
_____

Marriage gives you the opportunity to be brave enough to make your own choices and, knowing the consequences of those choices. Sometimes we think that the big choices, life's decisions, are the most important. List three big choices you and your spouse have had to make. List three bad choices. Where is God in your choices in life?

Your good choices:

_____
_____
_____
_____
_____
_____
_____

Your bad choices:

_____
_____
_____
_____
_____
_____

God has given you the **power of choice**. Our destiny is our choice. The Bible says, 'Your eyes saw my unformed body; all the days ordained for me were written in your book' (Psalm 139:16 NIV). Life is a series of challengers and sufferings. The reason for this is that God is more interested in our character than our comfort. You have the power of choice today. What are you going to choose?

There are times where you may find yourself at the cross roads, facing some difficult decisions and we're not sure which way to go. Have I made the right decision? It can be scary not being 100% sure I've made the correct decision. Do we marry or not? Do we quit our job or not? Do we move house or not?

Pause and Pray

'Lord, bless our marriage. Bless us with Your wisdom and discernment. Guide us in our decisions, whether big or small. May we always seek Your will above all else, and may we both make choices that reflect Your truth and love.

In Jesus name - Amen

Devotion Day 5. Purpose for Marriage

If your prime purpose as an individual is to be a representation of Christ on this earth, what is the purpose of your marriage?

Purity is a desire of the heart, before it's an act in the bedroom. First of all, sexual purity begins in the heart. I learned a powerful truth early on in my walk with Jesus, when we love God, we obey God. When I fell in love with Jesus my desires changed. Before, I was the girl hooking-up with guys and didn't think much about it. This was just normal … everyone did it. But when I began a relationship with Christ, something changed. I knew sex outside of marriage was not God's will for me and I wanted to obey. Not because it was a rule, but because it was right. Jesus said, '*If you love me you will keep my commandments*' (John 14:15).

Our hearts naturally gravitate towards that which we love. And when Jesus is our first love, then purity follows as a natural overflow of our devotion. When we believe God is good and His commands are for our good, then we want to put them into practice.

The purpose is this: God is love. Love isn't just something God does nor is it something He has.

It's simply who He is. Marriage is an institution of love, the first institution God established. Not only is marriage the first institution established by God, it is the poetic symbolism that He uses to represent the profound depths of His love for a commitment to us, His church, and Bride. The bride and groom are the picture of the Church.

A bride-to-be can stand motionless in front of the mirror for what appears to be an eternity. For any girl who has dreamt of this day, she can work hard to prepare for this very moment. Her hair can reveal a work of art, her makeup looks immaculate, never before has she felt so beautiful. Because of this beautiful symbolism, there is a greater and darker attack behind the assault against marriage.

A motive many are blind too and no longer recognise. They include attacks against marriage, its definition, its divine purpose and roots. It becomes more about politics and social progress. The Word of God makes it clear that we do not wrestle with flesh and blood, that our adversary is not a government or organisation.

'For our struggle is not against flesh and blood, but against the rulers, against the authorities, against the powers of this dark world and against the spiritual forces of evil in the heavenly realms'.

- Ephesians 6:12

There is an enemy working behind the scenes twisting and turning to devour what God created. He will not stop attacking marriage until he has completely distorted the framework of reference for the way God loves and relates to His people. The last thing Satan wants is for us to discover and receive God transforming and everlasting love. However, by the grace of God, we can defeat the enemy and embrace everything that our loving Father desires in our marriages. Not only did God make marriage, His plan and purpose for it hasn't changed. God still stands by His original plan. What does Jesus think about this?

> One day the Pharisees were badgering him: 'Is it legal for a man to divorce his wife for any reason'? He answered, *'Haven't you read,' he replied, 'that at the beginning the Creator 'made them male and female,'and said, 'For this reason a man will leave his father and mother and be united to his wife, and the two*

> will become one flesh', So they are no longer two, but one flesh. Therefore what God has joined together, let no one separate' (Matthew 19:3-6 NIV).

The Message Bible calls divorce a desecration of God's art. Its true - Marriage is God's art. Its something He created which makes divorce a big deal. Lets look at this further...
The meaning of the 'desecrate' is to treat something sacred with violent disrespect - or to soil. Terms such as insult, vandalise, blaspheme, defile and violate are all expressions that convey a sense of violence. Can you imagine how the world would respond if someone desecrated Claude Monet's *Water Lilies* or Leonardo da Vinci's *Mona Lisa*? Every newspaper, Television and social media stream would pick this story. The perpetrator would be frowned upon and condemned by society and would probably end up doing time in jail. How could anyone desecrate some of humanity's greatest works of art. The artist would turn in their grave's. God views marriage as one of the greatest works of art to be expressed through His favourite creation. His passion for marriage is evident in Jesus' response to the Pharisees. They soon discovered His words were too great for them to handle. Unable to comprehend marriage in light of God's original intent, they hid behind the

Law of Moses - an approach that gave them the license to leave rather than the empowerment to stay. Matthew 19:7-9 reads;

> They shot back in rebuttal, 'If that's so, why did Moses give instructions for divorce papers and divorce procedures'? Jesus said, *'Moses provided for divorce as a concession to your hard heartedness, but it is not part of God's original plan. I'm holding you to the original plan, and holding you liable for adultery if you divorce your faithful wife and then marry someone else. I make an exception in cases where the spouse has committed adultery'.*

Under the Law of Moses, concessions were made because of the hardness of the human heart. This became a provision, not Gods purpose. God hates the crippling effects of divorce. When a husband and wife are separated, one of the mysteries of Gods creation is violated and torn apart. Again, Jesus will never ask us to do something that He will not enable us to accomplish. He holds us to Gods primary purpose and plan for marriage because He's willing to equip us to live it. The Law of Moses made allowances for the hardhearted, but through Jesus' sacrifice we receive new hearts born of the spirit rather than of stone. There's nothing more annoying than a car that won't start when you need it to. It's easy to paint a dodgy car up and make it look good, while not bothering to fix, on the inside, what matters most. Although we try and try, why is it that we're not the husbands, the wives, the sons, the daughters, the friends that we could be and we should be. Perhaps, it's because we focus too often on the externals. For example: our behaviours, rather than on what matters most. Jewish teachers insisted on lots of ritual hand-washing. But Jesus taught that it's not the germs from the outside, but our hearts on the inside that cause our problems:

'The things that come out of a person's mouth come from the heart, and these defile them. For out of the heart come evil thoughts, murder, adultery, sexual immorality, theft, false testimony, slander',

(Matthew 15:18-19). Jesus taught that if our hearts are right, then our behaviours will be right. That's why the teachings of Jesus overwhelmingly focus on the heart. God isn't primarily interested in the externals.

He cleans you from the inside out. If your heart is right with God, the rest will follow.

Day 5 Devotional Questions
Purpose of Marriage

What is the purpose of marriage? The Bible has a lot to say about this topic, the first marriage was between Adam and Eve. The first reason that the Bible gives for the existence of marriage is simple: Adam was lonely and needed a helper (Genesis 2:18). The three primary purposes of marriage are, friendship, intimacy and a covenant.

What do you see in the character of Christ that you most wish were in you as well?

_____
_____
_____
_____
_____
_____
_____
_____
_____
_____

What are the top three qualities that first attracted you to your spouse?

1._____
_____
2._____
_____
3._____
_____

What three things now frustrate you the most? Is there any connection?

1._____
_____
2._____
_____
3._____
_____

(Be encouraged, your different answers are meant to unite - not divide)

What are your dreams and goals as a couple?
_____
_____
_____

The spouse God has blessed you with is a major contributor to forming you into the person you are today. Write down one positive change to your character or quality of life that has has an impact from being with your spouse. How is God using your spouse to enlarge your life?

_____
_____
_____
_____
_____
_____

Have you ever shown your appreciation by thanking your spouse for helping sharpen or adding purpose to your life? If not, its never to late to take time to sincerely express your appreciation. In a few words write down how much you appreciate your spouse.
You may consider the little things such as taking out the rubbish each night, or bringing the washing in when its about to rain. Think of some big events in your life.
I appreciate my spouse because…

Pause and Pray

'LORD, I BRING OUR MARRIAGE BEFORE YOU, ASKING THAT YOU WOULD NURTURE THE LOVE AND CONNECTION BETWEEN US. INCREASE OUR CAPACITY FOR PATIENCE, UNDERSTANDING, AND GRACE TOWARDS EACH ANOTHER.

IN JESUS NAME - AMEN

Chapter Two

Once upon a Marriage...

'This is why a man leaves his father and mother and is united to his wife, and they become one flesh'.

- Genesis 2:24 NIV

Devotion Day 1.

God's first purpose for creating man and woman and joining them in marriage was to *mirror His image* on earth.

Center your attention on those words, *mirror His image.* The Hebrew word for 'mirror' means to reflect God, to magnify, exalt, and glorify Him. Your marriage should reflect God's image to a world that desperately needs to see who He is. Because we're created in the image of God. People who wouldn't otherwise know what God is like should be able to look at you and get a glimpse.

Marriage is one of God's greatest gifts. A good marriage is a picture of Christ's love for the church and is a place of encouragement, growth, and grace. However, these kinds of relationships don't just happen. A strong marriage is not something that can be left to chance. Godly, mutually-edifying marriages are built intentionally, by the grace of God.

One of the most direct passages on marriage in the New Testament is Ephesians 5. This chapter provides a blueprint for how to cultivate a grace-filled, Christ-centered relationship.

The number of years in your journey together doesn't tell its full love story. A marriage of twenty years may reveal twenty years of hardship or twenty years of perpetual bliss. Yet, more often than not, marriage is a collage of varying and diverse seasons. When we look at the image of rings on the tree, every ring increases with diameter of the tree. Regardless of whether a year was one which held enormous difficulty or an abundance of joy. It all adds to the story and meaning to your journey. The challenges in our marriage have the potential to infuse our stories with similar excitement and meaning. Don't despise moments of discouragement. Use them to your advantage to draw on the grace of God and discover that His Divine strength will defy the limits of your emotional and spiritual growth.

Dr Tim Kimmel book titled *'Grace Filled Marriage'*, writes how only 10% of marriages which are truly positive and happy. The foundational reason for the holes in their marriages is the lack of grace. As Kimmel describes it, *'Grace desires the best for your spouse, even when they may not deserve it'*. Our marriages today are still learning new ways to show grace towards each other. We tend to bring our faults, failures, and idiosyncrasies into a marriage. However it is grace that communicates in word, tone of voice, and action. These challenges compelled us to rise and take a stand paving a way to be a testimony of Gods strength and grace in our lives. Your current struggles can become some of the greatest moments in your story. Once upon a time… your marriage was once a profound love story. Yet, what about the rest of us? What about the marital love stories and our happily ever afters we used to hear and read about. Our generation has witnessed our grandparents survive marriage and yet somehow throughout our generation it now appears all too convenient for each spouse to call it quits.

Once upon a time…marriage was forever. It still remains a covenant that knit one man and one woman together. This commitment makes both man and woman stronger, and nobler, There is without a doubt marriage is a wonderful, yet at times can be a painful process. Most of us tend to have a lot more patience than others with the pain of a process if we understand its full purpose. For example; you can endure a fews hours in a

Doctors waiting room, if you know the full outcome and purpose for your visit. In your marriage you have probably experienced moments like this. Days can be painful, like waiting in a waiting room rather to those walking along a sandy beach. Its in those painful moments that an awareness of your purpose is so vital. Today, the purpose of marriages is in question. Many people don't understand the purpose of their union, they are quick to end the journey what God delicately made since the end of time. They end up riding the turbulent waters and rocky boats.

Some argue how the whole entire institution of marriage is more broken than whole and it requires renegotiating, going from a covenant to a contract mindset.

Some even question that marriage contracts should be limited to a predetermined length of time - it seems forever is just to much to expect from any of us. People argue that it is unrealistic to make decisions about how we're going to feel twenty years from now and we can hardly control how we are going to feel tomorrow. There are others who want the definition of marriage to adapt with the times, 'Why can't we become more flexible'. If this institution is going to survive, it needs to expand further which includes unions of man and man or woman and woman. Certain celebrities are even refusing to get married until the parameters of marriage have been renegotiated.

(Let's stay true, each marriage should be growing and adapting, but the true definition and participants of a covenant union do not change). So, who do we listen to? Who holds the right to define - or re-define a marriage? Who holds the credentials and law to tell us how a marriage should impact our lives? We believe only God holds the right. His Word reveals;

'GOD, not you, made marriage. His Spirit inhabits even the smallest details of marriage. And what does he want from marriage? Children of God, that's what. So guard the spirit of marriage within you'.

- Malachi 2:15 MSG

There is no room for doubt. 'God, <u>not you</u>, made marriage'. Not only did He create marriage, but He is personally involved in the entire process of two people becoming one. Every marriage is made up of many different elements, some simple and some more complex. Yet, God brings to life the most intimate details by His spirit. God allows His creative expressions in marriage, but He retains all Creator rights as to what it is and whom it includes. Marriage cannot be recreated without His consent. The devil has tried to recreate marriage - he can only imitate Gods Holy creation.

The LORD declares in Malachi 3:6, '*I am the LORD, and I do not change*'.

Marriage is a miracle of God taking two people and making them one. As husband and wife, you create a single household. You pursue mutual goals. You share in exclusive intimacy. You join paths for a lifetime, devoted to one another's well-being. Nothing but death is meant to separate you.

Is anything or anyone coming between you today? Perhaps busy schedules are crowding out time to connect. Friends may criticise your spouse or make light of your commitment. Family members might compete for your loyalty. Job demands may steal energy and attention away from home. Your marriage might feel buried at the bottom of the pile, and you find yourselves drifting apart. Find your way back to each other today. Take courageous steps to put your relationship first. Confess what you've allowed to divide you. Recommit to loving one another wholeheartedly. Talk and touch, and give your undivided attention.

Remember why you love one another so very much.

Day 1 Devotional Questions

Once upon a Marriage…

God, our Almighty Creator of all, has given us the privilege of partnership with Him to reveal His character and bring His will and ways to the earth. This is true for us both as individuals and as married couples.

You and your spouse are God's Holy influential representatives to the world. He is revealing Himself through you both. Once upon a time you had a purpose to reveal to unbelievers to return back to Him. So, how appealing are you now? If you didn't know God and you saw a couple modelling their Godly example of marriage, what aspects or desires would cause you to be drawn to Him? What would turn you away or hinder drawing closer to Him?

_____
_____
_____
_____

When the Body of Christ reaches a point of not living or loving well to its full purpose, people blaspheme - use Gods name in vein (Romans 2:24). Is the Holy Spirit convicting you to make changes within yourself? Maybe an attitude or action of your marriage that doesn't represent God well. If so, what is it? What is being revealed to you?

_____
_____
_____
_____

(This is your personal opportunity to surrender to Him and ask for His help).

There are areas in all our lives where we have the opportunity to grow, learn and represent the Lord better than we should. Through the empowerment of the Holy Spirit we are able to accomplish this. As you both personally receive His love, you receive the ability to love your spouse and those around you. Read the following scriptures carefully and write what the Holy Spirit reveals to you about receiving and maturing in His unconditional love.

1. Romans 5:5

2. 1 John 4:7-17

3. Ephesians 3:16-19

List anything or anyone that maybe coming between you today?

_____
_____
_____
_____
_____

Complete the sentence:
I am remembering I love you because...

_____
_____
_____
_____
_____
_____
_____

Pause and Pray

'LORD BLESS OUR MARRIAGE. UNITE OUR HEARTS TO FEAR YOUR HOLY NAME AND WALK IN YOUR WAYS ALL THE DAYS OF OUR MARRIAGE, THAT WE MAY LIVE A FULL AND HAPPY LIFE TOGETHER. BLESS OUR UNION TODAY, AND ABOVE ALL, MAY WE HONOUR YOU IN ALL THAT WE SAY AND DO'.

IN JESUS NAME - AMEN.

Devotion Day 2. Jacob and Rachel

Jacob's purpose in fleeing to Harran was to find a wife. It did not take him long to fall in love. On the night of his wedding, Jacob finds that he is married to Leah instead of Rachel. Laban has played a nasty trick, and it will hurt his daughters as well as Jacob. But Jacob's favouritism will also take a toll, setting the stage for resentment and bitterness that will plague his family for a long time. It is easy to see the wrong in others. Jacob is quick to name Laban's fault. But Jacob seems to miss the fact that only a short time earlier, he had committed a similar deception against his own father and brother. We are responsible for the sinful ways we act, and we are more like Jacob than we might like to think. We get irritated when others do wrong against us, but we are quick to justify our own wrongdoing. Thankfully, God kept working on Jacob—and he keeps working on *our* hearts to.

Among the many love stories in the Bible is that of Jacob and Rachel, a tale of love at first sight, trickery, enduring passion and jealously. While on the surface it might not be easy to understand the deeper truth behind their complicated romance, it teaches us much about the vast and merciful love God has for each of us. From the start, Jacob in his youth is portrayed as a deceiver, which is what his name means. His twin Esau is a man of the land, a hunter, and the favourite of their father, while Jacob, who preferred to remain at home, was the favourite of their mother. Eventually, his mother helps him steal Esau's birthright and blessing, and Jacob flees his brother's wrath. This is where we meet Rachel, the beautiful second daughter of Laban, Jacob's relative in another land (Genesis 29). Jacob, by now humbled after his treachery and desperate for family ties and a place to call home, falls madly in love with Rachel. Rachel's older sister Leah was also unmarried, but their father, Laban, agreed to let Jacob work seven years for Rachel's hand in marriage (Genesis 29:18-20). Jacob's work for Laban wasn't easy, it was hard, gruelling labour. Jacob worked with Laban's large flock of sheep for the entirety of those seven years. He was more than willing to do this in order to marry his beloved Rachel. Indeed, the Bible tells us those seven years of labour *'seemed like only a few days to him because of his love for her'* (Genesis 29:20). Then, after seven years, Jacob was ready to receive his wife, Rachel, only to be tricked by his father-in-law. After the bridal feast, Jacob thought he was consummating the marriage with Rachel, but when morning came he realised he had been fooled. Laban had sent Leah in to lie with him (Genesis 29:23). Jacob, the deceiver, had become the deceived. When Jacob confronted Laban, Laban was resolute, in their culture, the younger daughter never marries before the older daughter. Jacob, as he had already laid with Leah, was stuck. But Laban told Jacob he'd give Rachel, too, as his wife if Jacob agree to seven more years of labour. Now Jacob had two wives, Leah and Rachel, both sisters, one he loved and one he did not. The outcome of all this was a love triangle that expanded to include the sisters' maidservants and many years of bitter jealousy and competition.

We know they lived happily ever after, but how? Jacob continued to prefer Rachel. God, as a consolation to the unloved Leah, enabled Leah to become pregnant with four sons in quick succession, Reuben, Simeon, Levi, and Judah. But He prevented Rachel from conceiving. In desperation over her barrenness, Rachel begged Jacob to lie with her servant, Bilhah, and thereby give her sons through this union (Genesis 30). Jacob agreed, and Bilhah went on to have two sons, Dan and Naphtali. Leah, not to be outdone, realised she had stopped bearing children, so she gave over her servant, Zilpah, to Jacob, and Zilpah bore two sons: Gad and Asher (v. 11-13). Then Leah became pregnant again and bore Issachar, Zebulun, and a daughter, Dinah.

Finally, the Bible tells us *'God remembered Rachel'* and allowed her to conceive. She gave birth to Joseph. Our lives play-out the same today as it did back in Jacobs day. The dynamics of relationships can be fruitful and flourish whilst others can be misleading, toxic and leaving you feeling drained and deceived. Just as Jacob put in years of hard work, so too is crafting your own love story. Its takes hard work. It takes effort from both couples. Jacob was so infatuated with Rachel, he idolised her from the very beginning, believing that he would only be happy if he could have this perfect woman. This idea still exists today. If we let another person be the source of all our energy and our joy, we are actually robbing ourselves of real joy that can only be found through the saving grace of Jesus.

This is the love story where God wins, because we see that pursuing Him first leads us to real joy and fulfilment. Just like Jacob, sometimes we only come to realise this after we have been through a mess ourselves.

Day 2 Devotional Questions

Jacob and Rachel

Despite their trials and tribulations, Jacob and Rachel's story is a powerful representation of love's endurance through time and difficulties. It's a narrative that resonates not just in its Biblical context but also in the hearts of those who seek a love rooted in commitment, faith, and unwavering dedication.

Who were Jacob and Rachel, and what can we learn from their story?

_____
_____
_____

How does the story of Jacob, Leah, and Rachel encourage us to trust in God's timing and plan for our lives, even when things don't go as we expect?

_____
_____
_____

How does Jacob's experience of being deceived by Laban relate to his own earlier deceit of his father, Isaac, and what are the lessons we can learn about the consequences of deceit and the importance of integrity?"

_____
_____
_____
_____
_____

There are many lessons we can learn from this story, but to me, it's the emotional undercurrent that I am most fascinated with. The rejection, jealousy, and the desire to be pursued are emotions that are still familiar in this modern day.

I am grateful for Jacob's and Rachel's story as it reminds me that what God sees as greater worth to the kingdom is not the outward beauty but the heart within. I like to take care of myself and, while I know that beauty is in the eye of the beholder, I also know that my body and physical strength will fade with time.

As we will see as this story unfolds, the sister with the more outward adornment isn't as strong on the inside as she'd hoped.

Jealousy is an ugly emotion and something that we all can, unfortunately, relate to. Jealousy can creep up into any type of situation and does not just affect one type of person more than another.
Godly marriages are meant to be like the tree of life, yet over time, for what ever reason we often harbour feelings of jealousy and bitterness either towards our spouse, family member, neighbour or work colleague. Search your heart and write down what ever bitterness or jealously you have in your heart. How are you dealing with it? Have you handed this situation over to God?

_____
_____
_____
_____
_____
_____

We are not be promised a pain free life. However, what we are given is so much more. Security in God's love, His pursuit of us, and the desire to use our lives for His glory can manifest into your love story that is far more special than anything you could see on the silver screen.

Describe the unique qualities you admire about each other. Talk about how God has especially designed you for each other. Share what you find appealing and attractive.

_____
_____
_____
_____
_____

Pause and Pray

'LORD BLESS OUR MARRIAGE. WE EASILY IGNORE OUR OWN JEALOUSLY AND BITTERNESS, YET WE GET UPSET WHEN OTHERS CREATE THIS AGAINST US. HELP US AS A COUPLE TO SEE OUR HEARTS AS YOU SEE THEM AND TO FORGIVE OTHERS AS YOU FORGIVE US'.

IN JESUS NAME - AMEN.

Devotion Day 3. Marriage, a Sacred Union

Marriage is a sacred union designed by God. It is a reflection of his love and commitment to his people. It is a covenant relationship that calls us to sacrificial love, selflessness, and mutual support. In a world that often prioritises self-gratification, marriage is meant to show the beauty of sacrificial love. As husbands and wives, we are called to follow the example of Christ's love for the church by giving ourselves fully for the well-being and flourishing of our spouse. Marriage is a journey of growth, forgiveness, and shared experiences. It is a partnership in which two individuals strive to understand, honour, and cherish one another. It requires open communication, vulnerability, and a commitment to work through challenges together. In the highs and lows of married life, we find opportunities for growth, grace, and deepening intimacy. In the context of marriage we learn to offer encouragement, extend forgiveness, and support one another's dreams and aspirations.

The concept of becoming one with Jesus in marriage is spiritual and mysterious. Yet, once its embraced, nothing is more practical for enjoying your marital journey. Faith is how union with Christ becomes operative and powerful in your marriage. If you are in Christ, this is now the defining truth of who you are. Your life, your story, becomes unfolded by another story. That's the way we define faith; faith means finding your identity in Christ. Your marriage has its own identity, its own fingerprint. To be found in Christ means you don't have to prove yourself anymore.

Your frantic attempts to find or craft an acceptable identity, or your tireless work to manage your own reputation, these are over and done. You can rest. Your marriage can rest. You no longer have to compete or compare or feel intimidated by other couples. Your marriage is in Christ!

Today let's honour the sacredness of a marriage union. May you embrace the call to love and serve your spouse, imitating Christ's selfless love.

'This is his command: to believe in the name of his Son, Jesus Christ, and to love one another as he commanded us'.

- 1 John 3:23

'Blessed are those who hunger and thirst for righteousness, for they will be filled'

- Matthew 5:6

What is God's will for your marriage?

The Bible provides a variety of images that help us gain some insight into this profound mystery. Jesus used a horticultural metaphor: '*I am the vine, and you are the branches. If a man remains in me and I in him, he will bear much fruit; apart from me you can do nothing*' (John 15:5). From this vital union with Christ we draw our nourishment, our strength, our spiritual life. Certainly our experience of the Lord's Supper is to be a visible expression of this union (or 'communion') with Christ.

Another way that you can understand your relationship with Christ comes through the Hebrew conception of the solidarity between a king and his subjects. When David was anointed as king, we read that all the tribes of Israel came to him to pledge their loyalty, and they said, '*We are your own flesh and blood*' (2 Samual 5:1). He became their leader, their representative before God. When King David sinned, as he did when he made a census of the people (2 Samual 24:1-15), the whole nation suffered. But when he was victorious in battle, the whole nation prospered. This notion of royal representation was then transferred to the solidarity of the Messiah with His people. When we turn to Jesus, in faith, and submit ourselves to Him as our King, we are joined to him, He represents us, and we become His own 'flesh and blood'. Believe in Christ and love one another. The two go hand in hand, binding you together in love and faith. Love without belief is limited and superficial. It's motivated by emotion, and lacks the depth and power only found in Jesus. Without belief, your love for self will overtake your love for your spouse. Your strength to forgive, serve, and sacrifice for each other will crumble without a foundation of truth. Marriage is a miracle of God taking two people and making them one. As husband and wife, you create a single household. You pursue mutual goals. You share in exclusive intimacy. You join paths for a lifetime, devoted to one another's well-being. Nothing but death is meant to separate you. God wants to transform your lives. He'll make you holy and pure. You'll be His shining light in a dark world. You'll receive the grace and love He's promised to give. As you receive the love of God through believing in Jesus, share that love with one another. Forgive as you've been forgiven. Give as you've received from the Father. Surrender yourself for the good of your spouse, as Jesus gave His life for you. Let Him fill your marriage with His perfect love today. Let's cultivate a spirit of humility, understanding, and compassion in our relationships. May your marriage reflect God's love and faithfulness, bringing glory to Him and serving as a beacon of hope to others in a broken world.

Day 3 Devotional Questions
Marriage, a Sacred Union

Marriage is a beautiful institution ordained by God. It is a blessing to be married to someone who saves... saves you from yourself. But seriously, being in a relationship with someone who loves and cherishes you is a treasure beyond measure. In Ephesians 5:25-33, the Bible describes the Biblical concept of marriage as a sacred union between a man and a woman, mirroring the relationship between Christ and the Church. Just as Christ loves and sacrifices for the Church, a husband is called to love and sacrifice for his wife.

What significant discoveries have you made about yourself? Think on what you've learned in your personal walk together. Talk openly with your spouse about the challenge this has been for you or the victories you have had. Write your answer below:

_____
_____
_____

_____
_____
_____
_____
_____
_____

Husbands, let's strive to be the men God has called you to be! Love our wife with all our heart, mind, and strength. Be their biggest cheerleader, supporting their dreams and aspirations. Wives, support and encourage your husband, being their helpmate and partner in every sense of the word. List three positive qualities about your spouse.

1._____
_____

2._____
_____

3._____
_____
_____

Marriage is a beautiful adventure, but it's not always easy. That's why you need to pray for our marriage, asking God to strengthen your love, your commitment, and your relationship.

What are your prayer points? Financial? Communication problems? Acceptance? Health? Family? Problems conceiving? Struggling to understand each others needs? List three prayer points below. This is the start of bringing your requests before God. These prayer points are something you can both pray on together.

Prayer:

1._____
_____
_____

2._____
_____
_____

3._____
_____
_____

Just as physical intimacy reaffirms your oneness, so does praying together. When you pray as a couple, you are not only communicating with God but also with each other. You can learn so much about one another by sharing prayer requests and listening to each other pray.

Read Ephesians 5:22 - 31, What analogies does Paul make between marriage and Christ?

_____
_____
_____
_____

Are these analogies encouraging to you? How/why not?

_____
_____
_____
_____

Pause and Pray

LORD BLESS OUR MARRIAGE, KEEP OUR HEARTS OPEN AND READY TO RECEIVE YOUR LOVE. MAKE US RIGHTEOUS AS WE SEEK YOUR FACE EVERY DAY.

IN JESUS NAME - AMEN

Devotion Day 4. Iron Sharpens Iron

Do you ever notice how people act differently after years of marriage? Constantly having to consider another person can make our wilder side grow a little gentler and give our compassion more depth. We all have some rough edges that need smoothing and polishing. We all have a few things to learn about wise living. We cringe at the sound of metal scraping on metal. We are used to our rough edges and are not always eager to let them go. To lose our jagged edges, we must have a willing spirit that is open to being taught. Are you willing to be shaped by your Creator? Marriage is one place where we share deeply of ourselves. In a good marriage your spouse will lovingly challenge you to live out your beliefs. Likewise, we value friendships in which we are loved enough to be corrected. True friends will speak the truth in love and help us become the people God intended. Often it can feel risky to challenge another person. We don't want to make waves or risk hurting a friendship, so we miss opportunities for growth and deeper relationships.

What Does 'Iron Sharpens Iron' Mean? When creating a metal blade, it is often sharpened, and then maintained through its life, by dragging it against a harder metal. Without this maintenance, a blade will become dull and less useful. During the life of Solomon, many weapons, pieces of armour, and tools were made of iron. It was also not necessarily consistent in how hard or soft it was. A tool would have been sharpened, ground against something harder, to make it smoother, remove deformities, and maintain its ability to cut. When iron is scraped against another material in this way, it becomes more refined. The metaphor in the first half of the verse refers to a common practice with which many would have been familiar.

The second half of the verse explains the metaphor. Like a piece of hard iron will sharpen another piece of iron, the interactions between two people will shape and change one another. Most scholars and theologians interpret this changing as a refinement of character. Being in the presence of a strong believer can help refine another person. Earlier verses in the chapter reflect this idea, *'Better is open rebuke than hidden love. Faithful are the wounds of a friend; profuse are the kisses of an enemy'* (Proverbs 27:5-6). An honest acquaintance will lovingly address when someone they care about is doing something wrong or struggling with a decision. It is also in alignment with philosophies of behaviour encouraged in the New Testament; *'Therefore encourage one another and build one another up, just as you are doing'* (1 Thessalonians 5:11).

Lets look at a couple of examples: A good chef knows a dull knife can be more dangerous than a sharp one. Although it seems contradictory, a dull-edged blade can actually do more damage to the chef, than the food! That's because when a blade is dull, it's harder to use. Not only does it take more force to actually cut something, but also it's harder to control. That's why a dull blade can slice a finger quicker than a tomato, and why chefs spend a lot of money on quality knives.

Every knife becomes dull with use. The sharp edge rounds out, and little chips develop. Cutting will render a blade ineffective, and on its own, it will never become sharp again. That's the first truth about sharpening iron: a knife cannot sharpen itself. Nor can something weaker than iron, sharpen iron.

The Bible uses a practical truth about sharpening iron, to teach a spiritual truth about our relationships with others: *'You use steel to sharpen steel, and one friend sharpens another'*. (Proverbs 27:17 MSG). We've all had the experience of friends who inspire us to be better than we are, and friends who don't. A godly Christian friend can sharpen you in areas they are strong. For example, a wise friend can make you wiser. A loving friend can expand your capacity to love. A Biblically knowledgeable friend can enhance your understanding of Scripture. Proverbs 13:20 says, *'He who walks with the wise grows wise, but a companion of fools suffers harm'.*

When we think of sharpening a blade, or sharpening ourselves, it's always done for a purpose. A chef doesn't sharpen a knife so it looks better lying on the kitchen counter. Sharpening is done to make it more effective and efficient. If we sharpen a knife for years and never put it into use, it will eventually be sharpened down to nothing, with nothing to show for all that honouring. We ought to apply this same method to our marriage. We are to be sharpened, and to sharpen each other, in order to advance the Kingdom of God. Whether we are talking about a knife, a sword or ourselves, sharpening isn't done for a passive activity. A blade is sharpened to accomplish a purpose. One reason Christians need sharpening is to be effective in the spiritual battle against sin surrounding us. (Ephesians 6:10-13) Proverbs 27:17 says, *'As iron sharpens iron, so a friend sharpens a friend'.* I believe the sharpening happens when we are intentional about how we interact with each other. Are you giving your spouse the attention they need or are you distracted by your devices? Are you applying pressure when it's needed to help move the other person. This sharpening happens a lot like the way you sharpen a knife. It doesn't happen without intentional contact, moving through life together, and going through some gritty times. Sometimes sparks fly, but you keep at it because you're making each other better. It's not always easy to do, but every one of us needs someone who will sharpen our lives and who will seek us out and lift us up when we're going through the wilderness. It's also critical that we are someone else's sharpener, who will bring encouragement at just the right time. None of that happens without intentionality. If you're feeling a bit dull lately, seek out that person who sharpens you and start the sharpening process. Remember, iron does not sharpen iron without friction and force. It takes effort. It's not always easy, but it's always worth it. Ministering to your spouse requires commitment, patience, and often a good deal of grace. It means extending love when it's hard, offering support when it's inconvenient, and always seeking to reflect Christ's love in your actions. Remember that each day is an opportunity to shape your marriage, to minister to your spouse, and to grow together. Just as the blacksmith takes the raw iron and transforms it into a useful tool with patience, force, and heat, so too can we take our raw selves and, through the friction and pressure of life, become sharper, more resilient, and more like Christ. Embrace the wisdom of Proverbs, and see your spouse not as an adversary but as a partner in refinement. Let your marriage be a place where iron sharpens iron, where both of you can grow, learn, and be shaped into the people God created you to be. In your marriage, be the minister, be the iron, and let the love of God, which is better than life itself, be the forge. We become better versions of ourselves as we minister to each other in our marriages. Growing in marriage is important. Choosing friends who will sharpen you is one practical way you can grow. God designed you both to embrace each other for fellowship, and for advancing His kingdom here on earth.

When we begin to view friendships in a God-glorifying, Christ-exalting way, then our friendships will truly mean something. Only then will you understand, what it means for iron to sharpen iron. You will begin to chase after holiness while helping your brothers and sisters do the same. Entering into genuine friendships is a declaration of war against our enemy, the devil. To not pursue friendships is folly and only leads to destruction.

Choose the hard road. Choose genuine friendships.

Day 4 Devotional Questions
Iron Sharpens Iron

The Bible strongly encourages that we develop friendships with other believers. In Proverbs 27:17, Solomon writes, 'Iron sharpens iron, and one man sharpens another'. Chances are that you've heard that verse before you may even have it on a men's ministry T-shirt or coffee mug but we often neglect to consider its implications. Solomon is saying here that friendship is a way to build others up by removing the crud. Iron sharpening isn't easy or pleasant work. It is dirty, hot, and dangerous. That is what friendship is like. When you begin to develop true, honest relationships, everything in the dark gets brought to the light.

Do you care enough about your relationship to correct your spouse with love?

_____
_____
_____
_____

We see this idea of genuine friendship modelled throughout the entirety of Scripture. From the bond between Jonathan and David to Jesus and his disciples, and even in the foundations of the early church in Acts, these relationships all point to authentic friendship. List a few names of your friends below. Do you consider any of them authentic? Who protects you? Who corrects you? Who do you trust? Who sharpens you?

_____
_____
_____
_____

Do you know someone that just rubs you the wrong way? Every time you meet, you clash. It seems like every time you're around each other, they bring out the worst in you. Then there are others you come into contact with who seem to make you want to be a better person. You have long, deep, conversations. They ask questions that keep you thinking for days.
You can't wait to be near them because they bring out the best side of you.

I think it's good to have both types in your life. I know it sounds crazy, but even the people who seem to bring out the worst in you can help you be a better person. List some personality traits you clash with? (For example; Laziness, impulsive, dishonesty, manipulative).

_____
_____
_____
_____
_____
_____
_____
_____

Now, list some personality traits that bring out the best in you? (For example; Happy, intelligent, caring, creative, giving, honesty).

_____
_____
_____
_____
_____
_____
_____
_____

What is one way you have changed for the better during your marriage?

_____
_____
_____
_____
_____

How can you help sharpen each other to become more like Christ?

_____
_____
_____
_____
_____

Pause and Pray

'LORD BLESS OUR MARRIAGE. HELP US TO HAVE A TEACHABLE SPIRIT SO WE CAN CONTINUE TO GROW IN YOU. GIVE US COURAGE TO CORRECT ONE ANOTHER IN THE CONTEXT OF YOUR LOVE'.

IN JESUS' NAME - AMEN.

Devotion Day 5. Contract Vs. Covenant

I'm no expert or theologian on this topic. However, it seems to me that understanding the powerful imagery of covenant is critical to understanding what marriage is all about. When your marriage is rooted in a covenant, there is a beautiful thing that takes place: your relationship becomes a *mirror through which the world sees God's desire to commune with His people in relationship.* A contract says '*what's in it for me'?* while a covenant says '*what can I give or sacrifice for the sake of the other'?.* Lets look at this example further:

Feature	Contract Marriage	Covenant Marriage
Basis	Conditions, mutual benefit and individual rights.	Love, sacrifice and faithfulness
Commitment	I'll stay only if you…'	I'll stay because God joined us'
End Condition	Can be broken when terms are unmet.	Life long commitment 'till death do us part'
Perspective	A legal agreement built on mistrust.	A sacred vow and a relationship built on trust.

When two people enter into a covenant together to combine two independently separate lives into one Christ-centered and shared life, there is bound to be tension! There will be moments of hardship, turmoil, and difficulty. If the relationship is based on a contract, then when a situation doesn't seem resolvable you will most likely execute the 'termination clause' and therefore the marriage relationship isn't worth fighting for because the foundation of the relationship was built on conditional statements and fulfilling certain requirements. A covenant also has requirements where each person fulfils their commitment to the other but there are no 'termination clauses' and **the foundation of the marriage is built on the Gospel.** The Gospel informs us that no matter what circumstances arise, the commitment to the marriage is greater than our desire to be right, or to 'win' the argument or to even be justified. You see, in the midst of us being mistreated, suffering, or dealing with a relationship problem, our tendency is to get revenge, lash out or resign in order to 'give them what they deserve' and that's exactly where the Gospel comes in. The Gospel leads us to overlook the faults of the other unconditionally because that's exactly what God did for us in sending Jesus to earth to suffer, die, and be raised to life again in order to provide a substitute, once and for all, for all the faults of mankind.

What if God responded the way most of us do whenever we are wronged, hurt, or betrayed? Let's just say it wouldn't go well for us! God is so gracious and loving that He not only overlooks our sin and waywardness, but took it another step further when He sent Jesus to forgive us of all our short comings, and purify us. Our response to our spouse, family, or friends in those moments of tension should mirror God's loving response to us at our worst moment. This is why marriage is so important and why it's important to understand that by making a covenant between yourself, your spouse, and God, you are promising to put God's love and grace on display in your personal life through your marriage relationship! What a great honour, responsibility, and privilege! I have been married to my husband for 14 years. I can honestly say that marriage is anything but easy. We both entered into our marriage covenant with a less than realistic idea of what would lie ahead of us. We thought, like many young couples do, that once we were married it would be nothing but endless fun and romantic blessings until death do us part! Now, don't get me wrong...we experience fun together, and continue to seek things that bring us closer together, yet those things are not the whole story. Along with seasons of joy and excitement, there have also been seasons in our life of intense pain, sorrow, confusion, health issues and fear. In those moments, ***you simply must have a foundation to stand on that is made up of more than just emotions and romance!*** What holds this thing together when the storms rage? We had to ask ourselves that question multiple times as we journeyed through life together and experienced a lot of things we never imagined would be so hard. It was in those moments that we came to understand the absolutely essential role of God in our lives, through the power of the Holy Spirit and came to rely on Him. Our foundation was shaken but not ruined because we both (individually and together) were putting Jesus at the centre of our lives and allowing Him to transform us, together, in the midst of our struggles and hard times in life. Once it dawned on us that God was seeking to transform us individually and as a family, we embraced the tension of life's ups and downs and began seeing that the more we embraced the tension, the more we were changed, forever, and for the better.

All of life, especially your marriage relationship, is an opportunity to let God turn the heat up on your life so that all the imperfections in you will burn off, rise to the top, be skimmed off, and leave you being a more refined version of yourself than ever before. This is all for His glory as well as your mutual joy as a couple and as a family.

'So God has given both his promise and his oath. These two things are unchangeable because it is impossible for God to lie. Therefore, we who have fled to him for refuge can have great confidence as we hold to the hope that lies before us. This hope is a strong and trustworthy anchor for our souls'. (Hebrews 6:18-19 NLT). Contracts have become such a common part of today's dealings, couples often fall into a trap of thinking their relationship with God is like a contract. If we pay with the proper obedience and devotion then God will, in turn, render the necessary service of providing answers to prayers or bestowing blessings. We fall into the trap with this mindset that, if we fail, then God will respond with judgment or a curse or mild irritations depending on the offence and its severity. You can hear it in subtle '*if … then*' statements. *If* I have more faith, *then* God will hear my prayers. *If* I stop swearing for a month then God will help me find a job. That is the language of contracts and God doesn't make contracts. He makes covenants. God makes covenants that rely solely on His holiness for fulfilment. He doesn't require anything from us but acceptance of the terms. They are eternally binding and utterly unbreakable. When Jesus makes a statement like, '*Most assuredly, I say to you, he who hears My word and believes in Him who sent Me has everlasting life, and shall not come into*

judgment, but has passed from death into life', (John 5:24 NKJV), He's making a covenant. We just accept the terms and it is irrevocable. When He says, *'I will never leave you nor forsake you'*. (Hebrews 13:5 NKJV), that's a covenant that we cannot undo, not with actions or words or attitudes. God knows our frailties. He knows that if our salvation, our blessings or any of His good gifts depended on our ability to keep up our end of a contract we would be left destitute. His boundless love and His infinite grace won't allow that. He takes all the responsibility on Himself. We just have to accept it. What should you do if your spouse is not living according to the covenant, they made with you on your wedding day? What if they are not loving you the way they are supposed to, or not treating you the way you think they ought to treat you? The answer is simple, but it is not easy. You made a covenant with God on your wedding day to fulfil your part of this marriage, no matter what your spouse does. Embrace and build your relationship on a foundation that truly can never be shaken, which is rooted in Jesus Christ. Follow Him and let Him transform and change you into the person He is making you to be and I promise you it will not be easy, but it will be worth it!

Day 5 Devotional Questions
Contract Vs. Covenant

The term **contract** is an agreement in which two or more parties outline specific terms, services, or goods to be exchanged. Contracts generally focus on discrete assets, services, or responsibilities each side promises to fulfil. In most legal systems, a breach of contract can result in well-defined penalties enforced by civil authorities. Contracts function primarily as legal tools intended to ensure fairness and clarity in transactions and relationships.

Just as God enters into **covenant** with His people, so too does He ordain marriage as a sacred covenant between one man and one woman. Like all other covenants, it is governed by God's commands for the sake of His glory and this glory is displayed as husband and wife are faithful to God's design for marriage. Marriage is an act of worship.

God offers to husbands and wives the highest possible significance for their marriage relationship by showing them what its greatest and most glorious meaning is —

namely, the replication in the world of the covenant relationship between Christ and his bride, the church. That's what the highest meaning of marriage is. There is no higher, more glorious, more significant conception of marriage than the one that Paul portrays in Ephesians 5, a parable of the greatest, strongest, deepest, sweetest, richest relationship in the universe — the blood-bought union between Christ, the Son of God, and his bride, the church. That's the meaning, that's the significance of marriage.

God designed marriage to be a lifelong covenant of companionship (Genesis 2:24). The Biblical ideal isn't merely that couples remain married but that they find great joy together (Ecclesiastes 9:9). Because God joins a man and a woman in Holy matrimony, marriage should be honoured and protected.
You must guard your own marriage from infidelity and neglect. You also must respect the marriages of others through both your actions and the counsel you give.

What actions can people see in your marriage that demonstrates you are in a convent relationship and not a contract. What stands out?

_____
_____
_____
_____
_____

The way people are viewing a marriage contract is shifting. Definitions of 'abuse', have caused the pendulum to swing. For example: Authority and Discipline is not abuse. It only becomes abuse when it leaves a scare or is done in anger.

Today both men and woman are quick to call it quits and file for divorce. There is little education or adequate preparation when uniting couples. As a result, some unhappy spouses give up on their marriages too young and too easily and divorce without Biblical grounds.

Do you believe neglect of marital responsibilities can be grounds for divorce?. What are your thoughts?

_____
_____
_____
_____

Have you ever felt like your marriage is more like a contract agreement? If so, How can you turn these feelings back to having a covenant relationship with your spouse?

_____
_____
_____
_____

Pause and Pray

'LORD BLESS OUR MARRIAGE. WE TAKE GREAT CONFIDENCE IN BELONGING TO YOU BECAUSE OF THE BLOOD OF THE COVENANT THAT SECURES US. WE STAND BEFORE YOU UNITED BECAUSE OF WHAT THE BLOOD HAS SECURED FOR US. BLESS US.

IN JESUS NAME - AMEN.

Chapter three

Old Baggage

'Come to me all of you who are weary and burdened, and I will give you rest'.

- Matthew 11:28

Devotion Day 1.

When you visit a big airport, one thing you're sure to see is baggage, passengers carrying all sorts of baggage, getting ready to fly, and their baggage gets loaded on the plane as well. There's an awful lot of weight in the bags, and airlines have strict rules about how much each passenger is allowed. But of course most of us try and pack in as much as we can and weigh the bags to see if we reach the maximum allowed.

I wonder if you're carrying too much baggage in your own life? What problems are you carrying around today? Are you carrying around baggage that was never yours to carry?

'Baggage' is the human condition. The question is how we deal with our baggage. Do we embrace it and learn from it? Or are we buried under by it, unable to carry it, and then resorting to ineffective coping behaviours that continue to hurt us? Or maybe you bury your baggage and emotions with an addiction. Human Baggage can be described as feelings, circumstances, or beliefs that get in the way. We have thoughts, worries, memories, and ideas that hamper our growth and slow down our progress, that's what baggage is. We take on a lot of unnecessary weight and suffer the consequences.

Jesus said in Matthew 11:28, *'Come to me all of you who are weary and burdened, and I will give you rest'.* How do you get rid of your baggage? You have to let go of it. Have you ever struggled carrying luggage while running to catch a flight or the bus, you know how difficult and exhausting it can be. Have you considered that the same could be said about carrying baggage from your past into your marital life?

Sometimes the burdens we carry have been with us since childhood. Painful experiences during those formative years can have a profound impact, even into adulthood. Things we saw, heard, or felt could negatively affect our spiritual life today. In fact, it's possible to be unaware of the load because after bearing it for so long, we may have become accustomed to the weight and bulk. Perhaps it even feels normal, but it's not what your Heavenly Father wants for His children. To run with endurance the course God has set for your life, you must lay aside these encumbrances. He can break any lingering unhealthy pattern and replace it with hope and deep satisfaction in Him. As you consider your background and childhood experiences, ask God to reveal the truth clearly. When you recognise ways in which others have had a negative influence, pray the He will give you a forgiving spirit and healing for any wounds that remain. Hebrews 12:1 reads, *'Therefore, since we are surrounded by such a great cloud of witnesses, let us throw off everything that hinders and the sin that so easily entangles, and let us run with perseverance the race marked out for us'.*

Are you carrying invisible baggage? Truth be told, the baggage we carry, is the invisible variety. Emotional wounds, offences, memories and entangling sin. This baggage, if we are honest, does weighs us down. If this baggage remains undetected and unexamined, it will hinder our progress in life, relationships and callings. People often say after a breakup, *'Let's start from scratch'.* Sounds nice, doesn't it? But the truth is, it's impossible? Not even your very first relationship started on a blank page. From childhood onwards, every experience shapes how you give and receive love. We live in a culture that urges us to "live in the moment", keep things casual, and avoid getting too attached. The result? People carry grudges and unresolved experiences, dragging around a heavy emotional suitcase from one relationship to the next. If you grew up watching your parents' marriage fall apart, it's easy to lose faith in love. Over time, defensive thoughts like *'marriage never works'* or *'you can't trust anyone'* can affect your decisions. But living in defence mode doesn't heal, it just delays the process. Your view of love is shaped by parents, friends, culture, and even social media. Unless we challenge those influences, we can slip into destructive cycles without noticing. The truth is, nobody goes into a relationship 'clean'. We all carry past hurts, beliefs, and memories that can affect how we relate to others. If we don't face them, conflict is almost guaranteed. Is it time to have a look at your baggage, throw out the things that are weighing you down and re-pack your bag? Running with perseverance the race marked out for you, is difficult to do carrying excess baggage. The reason you're burdened down is maybe you're still holding on to them.

Its time to let them go!

Day 1 Devotion questions

Old Baggage

So right now, in this moment, what baggage are you still carrying around? Are you carrying around baggage that doesn't belong to you?

_____
_____
_____
_____
_____
_____
_____
_____
_____
_____
_____
_____
_____
_____
_____
_____
_____
_____
_____
_____

How do you react when past baggage triggers emotional distress? For example:
(Do you revert to old coping mechanism)

_____
_____
_____
_____
_____
_____

How do handle conflict differently now, after dropping your old baggage?

_____
_____
_____
_____
_____
_____

Pause and Pray

'LORD BLESS OUR MARRIAGE. WE ACKNOWLEDGING OUR BAGGAGE. WE KNOW IT IS HINDERING US FROM BECOMING ALL THAT YOU HAVE MADE US TO BE. WE GIVE THEM OVER TO YOU AND TURN AWAY FROM THEM'.
IN JESUS NAME - AMEN

DEVOTION DAY 2. HANDLING YOUR BAGGAGE

God's Word tells us to '*Cast your burden upon the Lord*' (Psalm. 55:22). Notice that God does not automatically remove your burdens from you without your permission. He tells you to cast them on to Him. You action this. You place them into His hands. Hebrews 12:1 says, '*…let us throw off everything that hinders and the sin that so easily entangles*'. Here's an easy way to remember using *A-B-C*:

A – ASSESS YOUR BAGGAGE

Search your heart and pray that God would reveal to you the baggage you're carrying. Psalm 139: 23-24 reads: '*Search me, God, and know my heart; test me and know my anxious thoughts. See if there is any offensive way in me, and lead me in the way everlasting*'.

B – BEWARE OF BAGGAGE

Baggage can come from anywhere. Be aware of situations that cause you to worry or compare yourself. Also, beware of others' baggage. People are carrying baggage. You can sometimes see it in their attitude, choices, and words. Don't let another person's baggage create more of your own. I don't know what your baggage is, it's a personal matter. But there's no point denying it or pretending there's nothing there. Each of us has some baggage.

C – CHECK YOUR BAGGAGE

Leave it all at God's feet. Drop your bags and let Him pick them up. My favourite part: there's no weight limit. It doesn't cost more for a heavier bag. No matter what your struggles are, no matter your choices, your behaviour, it doesn't matter. Check your bags at the foot of the Cross and walk away. There's a wonderful verse in the New Testament, 1, John 5:3, which says, '*...to love God means that we keep His commands, and His commands don't weigh us down'*. This means God's ways for us are not out of line, they match our aspirations and personality. He knows what is best for us, and we can live each day trusting him for everything. When you prepare to travel somewhere, packing everything but the kitchen sink may sound like a good idea, but the truth is, packing light usually makes for a much more pleasant travel experience. The same can be said for the journey of life. Excess baggage makes life cumbersome and stressful. Everyone has baggage.

Day 2 Devotion Questions

Handling your baggage

Now, list how you are handling your baggage?

_____
_____
_____
_____
_____
_____
_____

Who (or What) are you turning to for help? Are you seeking advice? What emotions are revealed?

_____
_____
_____
_____

'For I know the plans I have for you,' declares the Lord, 'plans to prosper you and not to harm you, plans to give you a hope and a future'.

- Jeremiah 29:11

Would you be open to seeking professional support?

_____
_____
_____
_____

Are you solving the right problem within your baggage or are you just placing a 'band-aid' over it? (Temporary solution - never resolved).

_____
_____
_____
_____

Pause and Pray

'LORD BLESS OUR MARRIAGE. WE PRAY THAT YOU WILL HELP US TO BE MORE AWARE OF THE BAGGAGE THAT WE CARRY. HELP US TO ADMIT WE NEED YOU TO COME IN AND REMOVE IT. THANK YOU FOR LOVING US AND CARING FOR US'.

IN JESUS NAME - AMEN.

Devotion Day 3. Excess Baggage

There's a wonderful verse in the New Testament, 1 John 5:3, which says…

'*…to love God means that we keep His commands, and His commands don't weigh us down*'.

This means God's ways for us are not out of line, they match our aspirations and personality. He knows what is best for us, and we can live each day trusting him for everything. When you prepare to travel somewhere, packing everything but the kitchen sink may sound like a good idea, but the truth is, packing light usually makes for a much more pleasant travel experience. The same can be said for the journey of life. Excess baggage makes life cumbersome and stressful. Everyone has baggage.

Many people have what I call spiritual baggage. Maybe they grew up under some very bad teaching and kind of entered into a legalistic mindset or became incredibly judgmental. That's spiritual baggage. Maybe for you, you've got a bad feeling about church. Maybe you heard bad stuff about church growing up or you had a bad experience, so you don't like church and don't attend—that's spiritual baggage. Maybe your problem is with God. Life didn't turn out the way you thought it would and so you are angry with God. Or maybe it's that you're angry with other Christians. I know some who hate Christians. Just the name 'Christian' turns them off. Maybe that's baggage you are carrying. It's a spiritual baggage. Maybe for you it is relational baggage. You trusted someone and that someone you trusted betrayed your trust, so you have this wall up all around your heart and you won't let people in; you don't talk openly, and you don't allow yourself to become vulnerable.

You may be carrying around the baggage of abuse. Unfortunately, the statistics about the abuse that is going on in our world are absolutely and completely horrifying. Perhaps you know firsthand that kind of horror that abuse brings and what that does in your life. Abuse leaves us with baggage. And even though it wasn't your fault you need to name it. So many people have this self-image baggage. You know, I'll never amount to anything, and I'm messed up. I'm worthless. What about the baggage of addiction. Maybe you feel like you are hooked on something you could never ever break free of this addiction and the baggage just seems to enslave you. But we need to do more than just acknowledge that we have baggage.

We need to get specific about it. We need to acknowledge some truth about our baggage, because, think about it, some of our baggage is our own fault. Some of the baggage we're carrying around is the result of us messing up, us making stupid decisions. Doing things that we knew we shouldn't be doing. Some of that baggage that you're carrying around you picked up. It's a consequence for something you've done. You need to acknowledge that truth. It's possible you may relate to the words of David in Psalms 109:22, *'For I am poor and needy and my heart is wounded within me'.* So many of us carry wounds of brokenness and pain in our heart.

As we learn to give over our baggage to God, we will find ourselves much more at ease and much more joyful than we've been before. Others will be able to see our joy and it may cause them to want to let go of their baggage as well. While we will always have something to work on, I believe God wants to bring us to that place of satisfaction in Him alone. God knows we aren't perfect, He just wants our hearts. The more we can let go, the more we will let God in. We are all a work in progress, and God has great plans for each of us.

The results won't be instant, but if we can learn to submit to God in ALL things, we will find that this journey of faith is worth far more than anything in this world that we could ever hold onto. Excess baggage is expensive for life, it weighs us down. When we travel with excess baggage we are characteristically exhausted by having to carry all this extra stuff around. Most of what we have packed is unnecessary for our life purpose, but we packed it in, thinking it is required or believing we are not ready to leave it behind.

What is excess baggage? Anything you carry around that drags you down and prevents you from fulfilling your purpose. Usually, something that you should leave behind because it is not good for you.

What kind of excess baggage do we carry around?

1. The excess baggage of past relationships.
2. The excess baggage of hurts and disappointments.
3. The baggage of offences.
4. The excess baggage of a bitter spirit.
5. The excess baggage of secret sin
6. The excess baggage of rebellion.

The question then is, 'Did you pack that yourself'?

What excess baggage are you carrying around that is slowing you down, tiring you out, costing you, weighing you down, hampering you, and making you lose out on opportunities that are good for you? Excess baggage needs to be cleaned out. It means that we need to open our souls, take a good look and leave whatever is excess in our souls behind once and for all.

Hebrews 12:1-2 *'Therefore, since we are surrounded by such a great cloud of witnesses, let us throw off everything that hinders and the sin that so easily entangles, and let us run with perseverance the race marked out for us. Let us fix our eyes on Jesus, the author and perfecter of our faith'.*

Colossians 3:8 '*But now you must rid yourselves of all such things as these: anger, rage, malice, slander, and filthy language from your lips*'.

I Peter 2:1 '*Therefore, rid yourselves of all malice and all deceit, hypocrisy, envy, and slander of every kind*'.

These burdens can weigh us down, prevent us from receiving God's gifts, and keep us from seeing the needs of others. At the very least our baggage can distract us from the good things God desires to do in our lives. Once we place ourselves fully under the mercy and grace of God, we'll have no choice but to face what we've been holding onto. There is no shortcut for facing our pain, the failures from our pasts, our illusions about ourselves, or the ways we've misconstrued God.

God's presence and love are here for us, but the path to that presence will appear costly at first. We may have to go through some of the illusions and fears we've been afraid to face. We may wonder what we'll have left once we bring it to God in prayer.

On the other side of surrender is an opportunity for healing and mercy. Jesus described His mission on earth as that of a doctor, serving those who needed healing. That message is still true today.

Day 3 Devotion Questions
Excess Baggage

Letting go of old baggage, whether it's emotional, psychological, or physical, often involves acknowledging its presence, understanding its root causes, and consciously choosing to release it. This process can be facilitated by self-reflection, seeking support from trusted individuals or professionals, and practicing self-care techniques. Here's a more detailed breakdown of identifying and acknowledging your Baggage:

Self-Reflection: Examine recurring negative patterns, thoughts, or feelings that hinder personal growth or relationships. Consider what situations trigger these responses.

_____
_____
_____
_____
_____
_____

Root Causes:

Delve into the origins of your baggage. Was is a past relationship, a traumatic experience, or unresolved grief?

_____
_____
_____
_____

Impact:

Assess how this baggage affects your present life, relationships, and overall well-being.

_____
_____
_____
_____

Releasing the Baggage:

Forgiveness: Practice forgiving yourself and others involved in the past experiences that created the baggage.

_____
_____
_____
_____

Setting Boundaries:
How are you establishing healthy boundaries in relationships to protect yourself from further negative impact?

_____
_____
_____
_____

Support Systems:
Are you open to seeking support from trusted friends, family members, or a therapist to process emotions and develop coping strategies?

_____
_____
_____
_____

Letting Go:
Consciously choose to release the baggage, accepting that the past is in the past and focusing on the present. What steps are you doing to achieve this?

_____
_____
_____

Moving Forward:
Be kind to yourself throughout this process, recognising that letting go is a journey, not a destination. What does this journey look like for you?

_____
_____
_____
_____

By taking these steps, you can effectively let go of old baggage and move towards a more fulfilling and balanced life with your spouse. What burdens are you carrying today that need to be handed over to God? Is there any 'excess luggage' you need to let go of before starting the next part of your journey?

PAUSE AND PRAY

'LORD BLESS OUR MARRIAGE. THANK YOU FOR YOUR WILLINGNESS TO LIGHTEN OUR LOAD BY TAKING AWAY OUR EXCESS LUGGAGE. PLEASE HELP US TO WILLINGLY LAY ASIDE WHAT WEIGHS US DOWN AS WE TRAVEL THROUGH LIFE TOGETHER.
IN JESUS NAME - AMEN.

Devotion Day 4. Just in Case

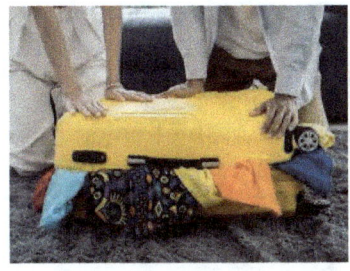

Look at the bags you travel with. Unpack them and look inside. What are you carrying? How long have you been carrying them? Do you carry a handbag? Maybe a small shoulder bag? Maybe you own one and have carried it around for years. I call it the 'just in case'. Perhaps you're familiar with this case, and possibly even have one of your own! Within this 'just in case' you hold things like, hurts, disappointments, resentments, grudges, old sinful patterns, negative thoughts, harsh and painful memories, and unhealthy relationships. Would you believe that within your case you even have a big picture album to keep faces of your offenders firmly planted in your mind's eye? To make sure you don't forget any of these things you have a computer inside your head where you keep an up-to-date record of the wrongs done to you just in case you might need that record to defend yourself. There's also an old tape recorder stored there so that at any given moment you can replay some of the conversations that have hurt you.

I must admit, many years ago this exact same case began to get very heavy for me. I knew there were things I was holding onto that God wanted me to let go of, yet, I had grown attached to them. I had to ask myself why it was so important to hold onto all of this baggage. The answer came with a rush of emotion in a conversation I shared with God. My 'just in case' had become so large that it was beginning to crowd the space in my handbag.

I presented my case to Him. Only this time the conversation belongs to you. It went something like this:

GOD: I knew that case would eventually get too heavy for you to carry alone. Show me what's in it.
You: Okay, God, but it's messy.
GOD: Let's see it anyway. Perhaps I can help you downsize a bit.
GOD: Why were you hanging onto all of this?
You: Just in case I might need it again someday.
GOD: Why would you need it?
You: Because I don't want to get hurt or disappointed again.
GOD: Do you trust Me?

You: Much to my embarrassment, God, I have to admit that there are obviously a few areas where I don't.

GOD: Do you know what the opposite of trust is, Doubt. Doubt is the soil in which fear grows. What are you afraid of?

You: I'm afraid that you won't protect or defend me when the time comes. I'm afraid of being hurt again. I'm afraid of being taken advantage of, abused, or taken for granted as I have been so many times when serving You. There have been times when I've been disappointed.

GOD: Don't you think I know all about this? I haven't promised that I'll never allow any pain or sorrow or hurt or disappointment in your life. Remember, I watched my own Son suffer at the hands of my children. He stood silent while they rejected and abused and betrayed and denied Him. And do you know why?

You: Why?

GOD: To accomplish my greater purpose. Trust Me for the bigger picture in your life too. Remember…'*I Am*'.

I Am your Defender. Trust that I have your back. Think of Job and Joshua, and Moses and David as they fought my battles. Trust that there are times when I'll ask you to stand firm in the battle and to remain silent. And other times I'll grant you the freedom to speak My truth in love.

I Am a Just God. One day I will right all the wrongs. Trust that vengeance is mine (Romans 12:19).

I Am Hope. Trust me when you have been disappointed and have lost your hope. Hope in Me does not disappoint. Others will let you down. Things of this world will let you down. And for the record, this world is supposed to disappoint you in order to remind you that you were made for another world (Hebrews 13:14).

I Am the Living Word. I have put my words in your mouth and cover you with the shadow of my hand. Trust that I will give you the words to say when the time comes. When they bring you to trial and deliver you over, do not be anxious beforehand what you are to say, but say whatever is given to you in that hour, for it is not you who speak, but the Holy Spirit. (Mark 13:11-13).

I Am your Redeemer. Trust that I have your best interests at heart. For I know the plans I have for you…plans to prosper you and not to harm you…plans to give you hope and a future (Jeremiah 29:11).

I Am unchanging amid all the change in your life. Trust that I am using the changes at and around you to transform you into My likeness (Romans 8:28-29).

I Am your strength. Trust that My grace is sufficient for you. In your weakness My strength will be perfected (2 Corinthians 2:19).

I Am close to the brokenhearted. I Am the Great Physician, Healer, and your Comforter. Trust me when your heart is broken. I save those who are crushed in spirit (Psalm 34:18).

GOD: TRUST ME.

You: Ok, I will.

GOD: Good! Now back to that 'just in case' that you carry. There's no need for that once you've learned to trust Me. There is no fear in love. But perfect love drives out fear…" (1 John 4:18).

You: Thank You for this reminder of who You are. I know that one day all wrongs will be made right. You will rise and every knee will bow and every tongue will confess that Jesus Christ is Lord. You will have the final word. Lord, on that day I will humbly approach Your throne and fall at your feet because I'll see myself as I really am, and I will see You for who You are. Father, I do trust that when you remain silent there's a greater purpose unfolding. With Job I declare, '*I know that my Redeemer lives*', (Job 19:25), and one day I'll see for myself that He rules the earth!

And there I rest my case!

Day 4 Devotion questions

Just in Case

Are you carrying excess baggage on your journey with Jesus? Are you refusing to check it at the gate of the Kingdom because you are so attached to its contents that you are fearful of leaving it in the hands of another? Is your life defined by what has been, or by what is, today? Remember, you are not the only traveler affected by your insistence to walking the narrow way with broad way stuff. Eventually you will become too tired to manage it all yourself and cease from traveling anywhere! To encourage us as one who certainly had 'baggage' in his life the Apostle Paul wrote:

> '...but one thing I do, forgetting those things which are behind and reaching forward to those things which are ahead, I press toward the goal for the prize of the upward call of God in Christ Jesus'.
>
> - Philippians 3:13-14

You can do it! **Check your baggage at the gate!**

What's holding you back? What's keeping you from moving forward?

___

Pause and Pray

'LORD BLESS OUR MARRIAGE. WE BELONG TO YOU. WE ARE A NEW COUPLE. THE PAST IS FORGIVEN AND FORGOTTEN. EVERYTHING IS NEW. HALLELUJAH! HOLY SPIRIT, EMPOWER US TO LIVE A BAGGAGE-FREE LIFE FROM THIS DAY FORWARD.
IN JESUS NAME - AMEN

Devotion Day 5. Ditch excess Baggage

Until you can acknowledge that painful things have happened to you things which were not appropriately finished you cannot work through them. And if you don't work through them, they will continue to disturb you in the present. So the first step to dealing with baggage is to confess to yourself and to God that you have issues that must be dealt with.

1. Include Others In Your Healing and Grieving

Seek from others the care and healing you need to finish whatever happened in the past. It begins with opening up your feelings to others about what happened in the past so they can comfort you, pray for you, and encourage you.

2. Receive Forgiveness

Often the pain we drag into new situations is from a failure in the past. In order to get rid of your baggage, you need to be free of the guilt and shame of past mistakes, failures, and sins. Once you know you are totally accepted, forgiven, and loved, you can tackle life with gusto.

Your past failures and mistakes may have alienated you from some people as well as from God. Your hurtful words or damaging actions may have made you a few enemies. If so, God's way for you is to go to those people and make it right. Humbly confessing your wrong and receiving forgiveness from those you have hurt is a vital step to leaving your baggage behind.

3. Forgive Others

Some of the baggage you carry is the result of being hurt or deceived by others. You may be the victim of a parent's lack of love and acceptance. Or perhaps you were betrayed by a partner, abandoned by a friend, dishonoured by someone, or misled by a spiritual leader. You were wronged in some way, and you still carry the pain, anger, and perhaps hatred from that offence.

If you are going to leave your baggage behind, you must forgive those who have wounded you. Take your cue from God, who has forgiven your sins. If you don't forgive, your resentment will continue to eat away at your heart and keep you from the freedom you seek on God's way.

4. Look At Yourself Realistically

You may have learned dysfunctional patterns for dealing with life, relationships, risk, and love, and these patterns are causing you problems now and holding you back from what God has for you. Take a close look at how you live. If you have trouble allowing people to get close to you, examine that pattern to see how it is limiting your relationships.

5. See Yourself Through New Eyes (Self Reflection)

Another kind of baggage we carry around is the distorted view of ourselves we learned in past relationships or situations. We see ourselves through the people who love us and sometimes through the eyes of those who don't. Our self-concept is a relational vision. We tend to look at ourselves through the eyes of others who are important to us. This is why some people suddenly blossom in healthy new relationships where they are valued as God's creation. It is also how other people grow to loathe themselves in relationships where they are devalued and mistreated.

How do you see yourself? Is your self-view realistic? Is it balanced with strengths and value as well as weaknesses and growth areas? Do you see yourself as loved?

6. Leave The Past In The Past

God's Word says in Psalms 103:12: *'How far has the Lord taken our sins from us? Further than the distance from east to west'.* Whether you had a troubled childhood, a bad marriage, or life has handed you everything on a silver platter, you have baggage. That baggage affects everything you'll ever do, every relationship you'll ever have, and every opportunity you'll ever be given. Allow a loving God to help you manage each day as it comes, in His strength, and not your own. Jesus offers to handle all situations that come our way. In the midst of this bracing honesty about our baggage, we can receive the affirming parental love of God. This is certainly disorienting in the moment, but it can ultimately lead to a sense of liberation. We may even feel like a weight has been lifted from our shoulders.

'Then Jesus said, 'Come to me, all of you who are weary and carry heavy burdens, and I will give you rest'.

- Matthew 11:28 NLT

Day 5 Devotion questions
Ditch Excess Baggage

When we go through difficulties in life with our baggage, the first thing we try to do is blame somebody else. But it doesn't matter where your problem came from, God still has a purpose for it in your life. Even when you do stupid things, God can use it. Even when other people hurt you intentionally, He can use it. Even when the devil plans bad things for your life, God can bring good out of it. Ditching your baggage allows God a greater opportunity to work in your marriage. Rick Warren's best piece of advice:

'God's purpose is greater than your baggage and your pain. God has a plan! You need to look past the temporary pain and look instead at the long-term baggage in your life'. God, in His grace, has made a way to get past your past. Remember, it is the accuser, Satan, who brings up the past. God is more concerned with our future. Today is a good day to give forgiveness a new start. Most people are stuck at the last thing they refused to get over. It is time to move on. In a few words, describe what your marriage would look like today if you were free from your excess baggage. Would you relate to each other differently?

___

'But God commands us, 'Forget the former things; do not dwell on the past. lest we miss the new thing He is doing right in front of us'!

- Isaiah 43:18

When we are facing problems in life, it can be difficult to believe that God has a plan through every challenge that we face. We can be tempted to believe that God is more interested in punishing us than in helping us. We can be tempted to believe that God would rather see us struggle than conquer. It can often seem as if our problems are running over us. We may even feel that the situation is completely hopeless and that we'll never recover from it.

Describe where you have seen God work in your life? Can you testify how God has freed you from any baggage? How are you helping others who may be experiencing the same situation?

_____
_____
_____
_____
_____

No matter how bad things look, God is always in control. A great verse in the New Testament, Hebrews 13:5 reminds us, 'Never will I leave you; never will I forsake you'.

We often bring 'old baggage' into a conflict. What can you trim or edit in terms of the baggage you bring to discussions about conflict in your relationship? For example: we romanticise the past. In other words, we think it was better 'then (whenever 'then' was).

We engage in the same argument again and again. So what part of your past can you leave behind to move ahead to a renewed understanding and space for positive discussion with your spouse?

_____
_____
_____
_____
_____

Prayer to forgive and release

'LORD BLESS OUR MARRIAGE. TODAY WE CHOOSE TO FORGIVE AND RELEASE ____ (NAME THE OFFENDER) ___ AND WILL NO LONGER JUDGE OR BLAME THEM FOR THEIR ACTIONS OR WORDS SPOKEN AGAINST ME OR MY SPOUSE. THANK YOU, JESUS THAT YOUR BLOOD CLEANSES OUR CONSCIENCE FROM ALL CONDEMNATION, HURTS, REGRETS AND DISAPPOINTMENTS OTHER WISE KNOWN AS OUR BAGGAGE'.
IN JESUS NAME - AMEN

Chapter Four

With This Ring

'That is why a man leaves his father and mother and is united to his wife, and they become one flesh'.

— Genesis 2:24

Devotion Day 1

Wedding rings are so much more than pieces of jewellery. They are symbols, reminders of love and commitment, visible testaments to a covenant made. When I look at the ring on my left hand, I see a reflection of the promises my husband and I made to one another, to love, cherish, and walk together through this life. But for me, a wedding ring doesn't just represent my earthly marriage; it also points to something greater. Your wedding ring tells a story.

The ring on my left hand symbolises my covenant with my husband. It reminds me daily of the blessing of marriage and the call to reflect Christ's relationship with His church. Ephesians 5:25-33 beautifully captures the profound mystery of this union, likening a husband's love for his wife to Christ's sacrificial love for His bride. Through the ups and downs of life, marriage teaches us about God's patience, care, and unwavering commitment. It's an earthly covenant, one that binds two people together until death parts them. This ring is a precious reminder of the temporal gift of love God has given me in my husband, a love that mirrors, in part, the far greater love of Christ.

The ring on my right hand holds a different meaning. It reminds me of my eternal covenant with God. While my earthly marriage is for this life, my relationship with the Lord endures forever. Isaiah 41:13 speaks to my heart when it says, *'For I, the LORD your God, will hold your right hand, saying to you, 'Fear not, I will help you'.* I picture God's steady hand holding mine, guiding me, comforting me, and assuring me of His presence. This ring is a tangible reminder that God's promises are unshakable. Even when everything else fades, He will never let go of my hand. When I wear these two rings, I am reminded that both my hands are held. My left hand points to the temporal covenant I share with my husband, a gift that reflects God's design and goodness, his love, provision and protection through him. My right hand points to the eternal covenant I have with Christ, the foundation of my life and the source of all hope. These rings speak to me of faithfulness, my husband and mine, but more importantly, Christ's faithfulness to me and my own commitment to Christ to love, honour and serve Him for all eternity. Together, they tell the story of love that is both temporal, eternal and complete. One day, the ring on your left hand will be no more. Death will separate you both as it does for all earthly marriages. But the covenant symbolised by the ring on my right hand will endure. God will still be holding my hand, leading me safely home. This truth gives me comfort, courage and strength because I know the One who holds my right hand will never let go. So, I wear these rings as a testimony, a visible reminder of two covenants: one for this life and one for eternity. They remind me to live faithfully, to love deeply, and to trust fully in the God who has given me both temporal and eternal blessings. Both hands are held, and I am never alone, secure in the grip of His enduring faithfulness.

Are you standing for the restoration of your marriage? Should you keep wearing your wedding ring?

In the marriage ceremony, after the vows are said, the minister solemnly and reverently remarks, 'What God has joined together let no man seperate'. Is not God the third part in a marriage? Should He not be taken into account in the marriage, and in the home that emerges from that marriage? If God joins the couple together at the outset, should not His presence be recognised in the home continually?

Many homes are on the rocks today because God has been left out of the domestic picture. With the clash of personalities in a domestic pattern, there must be an integrating force, and the living God is that Force! Many couples think that if they have a better home, get a better job, or live in a different neighbourhood, their domestic life will be happier. No! The secret of domestic happiness is to let God, the third part in the marriage covenant, have His rightful place in the home.

Make peace with Him, and then you can be a real peacemaker in your home.

DAY 1 DEVOTION QUESTIONS
WITH THIS RING

What does an engagement ring mean to you? Where was the proposal?

_____
_____
_____
_____
_____
_____
_____

What is your understanding on the wedding ring? Would you accept a family heirloom?

_____
_____
_____
_____
_____
_____
_____

When would you give your spouse an eternity ring? On your first wedding anniversary or the birth of your first child?

_____
_____
_____
_____
_____
_____

Where do place your value? In the price, the design or the symbolic meaning?

_____
_____
_____

Pause and Pray

'LORD BLESS OUR MARRIAGE. AS THESE RINGS ENCIRCLE OUR FINGERS, MAY YOUR DIVINE AND CONSTANT LOVE ENCIRCLE OUR HEARTS. THANK YOU THAT THE VALUE OF OUR RINGS FAR SURPASSES THAT OF GOLD AND DIAMONDS. MAY THE BLESSINGS AND POWER OF THE HOLY SPIRIT BE UPON US.

- IN JESUS NAME - AMEN

Devotion Day 2. The Wedding Ring

The wedding ring is perhaps the most recognisable symbol of marriage. Wedding rings are meant to last forever a timeless symbol of love and commitment. They are often passed down from generation to generation, becoming heirlooms of priceless significance, within each of the stories of those who once wore them. But what about the story of the wedding rings themselves? To understand their intricacies, we first need to rewind the history of mankind… by a few millennia.

The story of the wedding rings begins in the part of the world that is also credited with the birth of human civilisation. There is archaeological evidence that the first known use of wedding rings occurred about 6,000 years ago in ancient Egypt. Relics indicate that Ancient Egyptians saw rings – woven rings, made of natural materials such as reeds, hemp, or leather – as a token of love from husband to wife. A ring is a circle, after all, and the ancient Egyptians considered the circle to be a symbol of eternity. Since a circle has neither beginning nor end, it symbolised eternal love and the never-ending bond of marriage. Traditionally, the wedding ring is worn on the fourth finger, also called the ring finger, of the left hand. This is because the ancient Egyptians believed that there was a artery on this finger that was directly connected to the heart.

Other civilisations adopted this custom and carried it forward. The Greeks and later the Romans were also enthusiastic about the rule of the fourth finger.

The Romans even began to call it vena amoris (love vein). Their wedding rings were usually made of ivory, bone, or iron. They believed that durability was a better representation of permanence, and called the rings annulus pronubus (bridal ring). The Romans were also the first to have their rings engraved. Feather rings, for example, showing engravings of two interlocked hands, became very popular. Early Roman law recognised three types of marriages, called *confarreatio, usus,* and *coemptio*. In confarreatio marriages – 'marriages in the elite class' – rings of silver and gold were exchanged, but they still symbolised ownership and possession. Roman men 'claimed' their wives by giving them a ring and refused to wear one themselves. Later, wedding ring traditions were incorporated into Christian wedding ceremonies in the European middle ages. Early Christian rings, however, were so heavily engraved and styled that the church at the time denounced them as too elaborate. This led to the adoption of plainer styles, similar to the wedding rings that are widely used today. But extravagance is making a comeback with the the popular two interlocking bands.

After the engagement, the bride and groom-to-be each wore one piece. At the wedding, the groom put his ring on the bride's finger and rejoined the two parts. Poetry rings (with short engraved poems or scriptures) made of plain sterling silver were also common. The inscriptions, usually facing inward, show that couples began to view marriage as something personal and intimate, rather than just a legal agreement

During The World War II, soldiers on active duty began wearing wedding rings to remind them of their wives back home. Until then, it wasn't very common for men to wear wedding rings. That's right: while the wearing of wedding rings by brides can indeed be traced back to ancient Egypt, there is little evidence that until the second half of the last century more than a small minority of grooms did the same. Today, however, it is standard for both couples to wear a wedding ring as a tangible symbol of the permanent place their spouse holds in their heart. In many cultures it's now considered normal to wear the ring on the right hand. However, it remains customary for the wedding ring to be placed on the ring finger of the *left* hand during the wedding ceremony. But while some things may have changed with the times, one hasn't: the symbolism of the wedding ring.

The symbolism of the wedding ring is closely related to the symbolism of its shape: the circle. The circle is a universal symbol with extensive meaning, best known for representing unity, infinity, eternity, and utmost perfection. In fact, symbols based on circles can be found in virtually every chapter of human history. In the Christian faith, as well as in many other religions, circles are also seen as symbols of God, since they have no beginning and no end. This has made rings, especially wedding rings, symbols not only of love, but of eternal love. What could be more romantic than the concept of two small circles that will accompany you throughout life, as a symbol of your bond and the everlasting and enduring nature of your love?

Traditionally, wedding rings are plain and made of high-quality precious metals such as gold or silver, but there is nothing wrong with embellishments such as engravings and gemstones that have symbolic powers. Romantics have engraved their wedding rings with poems that have meaning to them. Many couples today adorn their wedding rings with meaningful dates, symbols, initials, poems and song lyrics. And when it comes to combining gemstones with precious metals to create stunning wedding and engagement rings, diamond – considered the hardest of substances – remains the most popular choice: the perfect metaphor for the promise that the bond of marriage represents.Scripture provides examples of rings used in meaningful ways. Genesis 41:42 describes Pharaoh bestowing a ring upon Joseph, indicating honour and responsibility. In the parable of the prodigal son, the father says, *'Put a ring on his finger'* Luke 15:22, showing acceptance, restored relationship, and familial bond. While these references are not specifically about wedding rings, they demonstrate that wearing a ring can represent a deep, Holy commitment. Conversely, the Bible also warns believers not to focus excessively on external adornment. In the book of 1Peter 3:3 teaches, *'Your beauty should not come from outward adornment'.* reminding Christians to keep the heart's devotion to God at the forefront. Consequently, wedding rings, like any physical adornment, must be considered in light of whether they help or hinder a believer's walk with God. Jesus had an inner circle. The Bible offers plenty of examples. As a matter of fact, He had several circles or rings of relationship around Him.

Consider the rings of relationships that gravitated around Jesus as He walked this planet. I call them the 'Rings of the Lord' or the 'Circles of Christ'. An overview of the Gospels shows there were at least six identifiable groups around Jesus:

The Crowds - The outermost ring of association with Jesus and the first one we come to is the Crowds. Crowds started to gather around Jesus early in His ministry.

Five Thousand - The Five Thousand did more than observe and evaluate Jesus as He touched and helped them. This group followed Him into the desert, desperate not to miss even one of His miraculous works of healing or provision (John 6:1-15).

Seventy (or some versions translate this as the Seventy-two):

Next were the Seventy. Out of the larger groups, a select team rose up to share in Jesus' ministry. You might say these people left the ring of observation and entered the ring of participation. The Seventy would do the same works they had seen Jesus do.

The Twelve: The ring most familiar to us is the Twelve, Jesus' beloved band of brothers, His chosen disciples:

'One of those days Jesus went out to a mountainside to pray, and spent the night praying to God. When morning came, He called His disciples to Him and chose twelve of them, whom He also designated apostles' (Luke 6:12-13, emphasis added).

Christ called this 'Shepherd's dozen' to leave all they had and follow Him.

The Three: One of the innermost circles around Jesus was His cabinet of three, (Peter, James and John). Church history respectfully dubbed this ring the Triumvirate. Triumvirate is a Latin term that refers to a powerful team of three individuals. Of all Jesus' disciples, there were three who saw, heard, and experienced the most.

The One: Ultimately only one person bears the distinction of having been the closest person to Christ during His earthly ministry. I like to think of this person as the 'one', the closest one, (John). This person sat at right next to Jesus at the Last Supper. He listened closer to Jesus' words than anyone else and, as a result, recorded more of them than anyone else. He was the go-to man when Jesus' disciples had a question they wanted to ask Him. He spotted Jesus on the shore when no one else in the boat recognised Him. He followed Christ to at least one place no other among the Twelve would go. Each group represents a circle or ring of relationship to the Lord, six stages or areas in relationship to Jesus Christ. They represent places to which people came and experienced Him.

Make no mistake, there is one place and one place alone to which Christ wants you to be when it comes to Him, and that is close. It's true, the devil is selling you a lie that relationships and friendships are made from more *likes*, more Facebook friends, more followers, more retweets, more TikTok. Yet, sadly couples are lonelier than ever before, and we are more depressed than ever before. Why? Because we do not have human contact like Jesus wants us to. Mother Teresa once said, 'The most terrible poverty is loneliness, and the feeling of being unloved'. Always surround yourself with friends and family that rally around, not come between, you and your spouse. Granted, if you aren't married, and your friends and family are shouting out warning and cautions to you, don't ignore them as though they just want to destroy your relationship. Before marriage, I would definitely encourage you to listen to the things that those who care about you are saying. They are speaking out of a genuine and sincere place, and it might be something that you are blind to because of your feelings for him/her. Regardless, make sure that the people you are letting into your inner circle of your life are people who should be there. They should be individuals that value and cherish you as well as your marriage. It all starts...'*With this ring'*

Day 2 Devotion Questions
The Wedding Ring

Getting married is one of life's biggest milestones, so it's no surprise that many couples want to ensure they're on the same page before walking down the aisle. Below are a few light-hearted questions to share with your spouse. These conversations can help you explore everything from values to life goals.

Why do you want to get married? Why is marriage so important to you?

_____
_____
_____
_____
_____
_____
_____
_____

Are you influenced by your parents' marriage?

_____
_____
_____
_____

How do you deal with change or the unexpected?

_____
_____
_____
_____

Do you both want children? How many? What if having children isn't straightforward?

_____
_____
_____
_____

Pause and Pray

'LORD BLESS OUR MARRIAGE. GRANT US GRACE, POWER AND THE STRENGTH TO DO THE FATHER'S WILL FOR THE REST OF OUR LIVES'.
IN JESUS NAME - AMEN.

Devotion Day 3. Love is a Sacrifice

Marriages never stand still. When my husband and I were engaged, we read several marriage books to understand God's definition on love. Both of us had a past of unhealthy relationships. What was love supposed to look like in a marriage?

In Ephesians 5:25-26, God reminds us marriage is supposed to represent the love Jesus has for the church. God showed us what love is by sacrificing His Son to die on the cross for us.

Love is a sacrifice, where we sacrifice our own needs and wants for the other person. Sacrificial love is also known as *agape* love, where we serve the other person, unconditional without expecting anything in return.

1 John 3:18 illustrates that we are called to love with actions and in truth, and not just words or speech. We can say we love our spouse, but if we don't show love by our actions, our words mean nothing. Sacrificial love in any relationship, be it with a parent, sibling, spouse, boyfriend/girlfriend, or or friend means loving the other person with good intentions, good actions, and

with no regards to yourself. Sacrificial love can be restricted or restrained by what you are willing to sacrifice in that relationship. Being afraid to love certainly affects the other people in our life. We may be allowing ourselves to hold back love based on fear of rejection, codependency, unrequited love, or for other reasons. 1 John 4:18 reads: *'There is no fear in love. But perfect love drives out fear, because fear has to do with punishment. The one who fears is not made perfect in love'*. We have to look beyond our own emotions or feelings and love others regardless of what we fear or consider to be faults or sins in another person's life. *'If we claim to be without sin, we deceive ourselves and the truth is not in us'*
(1 John 1:8).

Therefore, we have to remember just as God has forgiven and will forgive us, when we humble ourselves and ask, we need to forgive and continue to forgive others.

Love happens on an individual basis and rarely at the same time. One rarely notices when they may have failed to give sacrificial love in their relationship. However, it becomes easy for us to recognise or feel we haven't received love. We start noticing small things that aren't reciprocated and make them big things. We notice if someone never says *'I love you'* first.

We notice if a person doesn't wait up for us. We notice if they never cook or buy us dinner. We know when our needs have not been met or when we are being treated differently than how we treat the other person. This can create a spiral, and we can become consumed with thinking *'what about me'?*

When you sacrificially love in a relationship, you are making a choice to honour and respect the other's thoughts and feelings. You need to treat their feelings as if they were your own. You include their needs and desires in your actions. You learn to grasp a sense of honour and pride that comes from loving them. *'No one has ever seen God; but if we love one another, God lives in us and his love is made complete in us'* (1 John 4:12 NIV). I've experienced love through the peak of our 'honeymoon' phase, but I've never felt more loved through pregnancy and motherhood.

My husband has supported me through many things in life. He has held my hand through many doctors appointments, He prayed over our pregnancy, He talked to our baby whilst still in the womb. After our son was born, my husband played and interacted with our son so I could rest. My husband was not afraid to change a loaded nappy or clean up baby vomit. He would sacrifice his sleep to nurse our son, so I could get a good nights rest. To this day, He still helps out with cooking, helping with homework and playing with our son. Its easy to love your spouse on date nights or romantic holidays away. But true sacrificial love is found in our actions, especially when its inconvenient. The Greek word for this sacrificial love is *agape*. 'Unconditional love that is always giving and impossible to take or be a taker. It devotes total commitment to seek your highest best no matter how anyone may respond. This form of love is totally selfless and does not change whether the love given is returned or not'. Think how many times you have been forgiven for something, especially when you have really hurt someone. That act of forgiveness is a sacrifice, a dying to self so that in love, there can be healing. Oh, none of this is easy. Loving others, loving yourself never is, though recognise that, in a personal sacrifice, you make the world a better place. In and through that act, that showing of love, you encourage and enable others to experience love and emulate your actions. Jesus doesn't expect anything in return. He loves you when you speak and spend time with Him daily, spend time in His Word.

'UNCONDITIONAL LOVE IS GIVING THE OTHER PERSON WHAT THEY NEED THE MOST, WHEN THEY DESERVE IT THE LEAST, AT GREAT PERSONAL COST TO YOURSELF'.   - CHIP INGRAM

DAY 3 DEVOTION QUESTIONS
LOVE IS A SACRIFICE

What do you think love should look like in a marriage?

_____
_____
_____
_____
_____
_____
_____

How do you see sacrificial love displayed between couples around you?

_____
_____
_____
_____
_____
_____
_____

How do you show sacrificial love in your relationship?

_____
_____
_____
_____
_____
_____

How do you see God's sacrificial love in your marriage?

_____
_____
_____
_____
_____
_____

Pause and Pray

'LORD BLESS OUR MARRIAGE. THANK YOU FOR SHOWING US WHAT LOVE IS THROUGH YOUR SON JESUS. SHOW US HOW TO LAY DOWN OUR LIVES FOR EACH OTHER AND HOW TO LOVE EACH OTHER EVEN WHEN ITS HARD.

IN JESUS NAME - AMEN

Devotion Day 4. Relationship with God

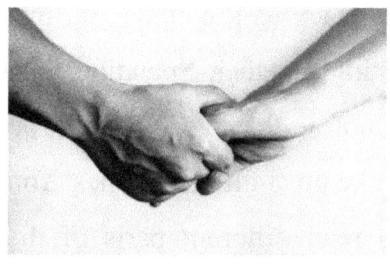

God answered my prayer for a man who loved Jesus, but I still needed alone time with God. Would my husband want to read the Bible with me? Pray with me? Would he understand I wanted to pray by myself sometimes? You have finally met someone to share your life with. If you love God with all your heart, you already know how important it is to marry someone who loves the Lord. But, what does a relationship with God look like as a married couple?

If you desire your marriage to last forever, God should be the centre of your marriage. Growing closer to God will strengthen your marriage, but it's also important to maintain and establish your own personal relationship with God. Remember your spouse is not your Holy Spirit. When we face problems and challenges, God should be the first person we turn to. Expecting your spouse to solve your problems puts pressure and unrealistic expectations on your marriage. While its healthy to confide in your spouse so they can pray for you, its still important to rely on God as your Heavenly Father. It all starts…with this Ring! As you get married, you'll establish routines to grow your spiritual intimacy as a couple. But this doesn't mean you will do everything together. Spending time with God together everyday may not be feasible for you. You may be conflicting schedules or wake up at different times. You and your spouse may choose to read different parts of the Bible. If you only have one thing to do together with your future spouse, I encourage you to pray together. Prayer is the most powerful thing you can do for your marriage as you share your heart with each other and with God.

Your relationship with God is unique. How your spend time with God may look different from your spouse. Both of you seeking God is what matters. God designed marriage not as a trial to be endured, but as a pointer to and catalyst for your greatest joy. God didn't design marriage to be your storybook ending, but a fresh beginning, to help get you ready for the true *'happily ever after'* when together we see our great Bridegroom face to face. When we remember that God is always present, all the Scripture verses about how to treat each other take on an added importance. With His presence at the centre of our relationships, we can transform our marriages. Being more aware of God's presence has led me to focus on having a more God-ordered marriage. I ask myself different questions than I used to. I often end the day by thinking, *Am I ok with how my husband treated me today? Am I happy with my marriage?* With God at the centre of our marriage, I now often reflect on, *How does God feel about the way I'm treating His son (my husband)?*

God knows that on our own we can't love the way He calls us to love. Furthermore, He doesn't even expect us to. But He does want us to go to Him, lean on Him and learn to let His power course through our sinful hearts and minds so that we can be of influence to others who take notice. By putting God's presence at the centre of your marriage, you are able to enlist His help to love. God made marriage for the deepest level of human community, a husband and wife should cultivate friendship together. No marriage can skip this step. In the most romantic book in the Bible, a bride says of her husband, *'This is my beloved and this is my friend'* (Song of Solomon 5:16). A husband and wife are much more than friends, but they should maintain the strongest of friendships together.

The main question we should ask ourselves is: 'What is the Biblical vision for having a relationship with God? It is not enough to have a vision for marriage. Everyone has one. But what we want is a Biblical, scripturally-sanctioned, God-ordained, Spirit-breathed, divinely-designed vision for marriage. Jesus said the house built on His word would stand, but the house built without His word would crumble (Matthew 7:24-27). My passion is to see marriages stand the test of time, marriages built on the rock of Christ. So, what is the Biblical vision for your marriage? Lets look at a few examples:

The 'Espresso shot' relationship with God
- Our relationship with God is like a quick jolt of caffeine when we need it, but we rarely slow down long enough to give him our hearts.

The 'What's yours is mine' relationship with God
- We base our relationship with God on other people's faith. Whether it's through church sermons or conversations with friends, our faith is fully dependent on the faith of others.

If you want to transform your relationship, consider how you can make God's presence the centre of your marriage. To have a close relationship with God, you need to not only serve Him with your actions, but also with all your thoughts and with a complete heart.

DAY 4 DEVOTION QUESTIONS
RELATIONSHIP WITH GOD

As you think about your relationship with God, it's important to ask yourself how you are treating Him in return. If God is inviting you into a wonderful friendship, how have you been responding?

How do you spend time with God throughout the week?

_____
_____
_____
_____

How much energy and effort are you putting into your relationship with God?

_____
_____
_____
_____

How do you want to seek God together as a couple?

_____
_____
_____

How can you make God a priority in your schedules?

_____
_____
_____

Are you giving God all of your heart, mind, and strength?

_____
_____
_____

How much does God's Word influence your heart?

_____
_____
_____

Pause and Pray

'LORD BLESS OUR MARRIAGE. YOUR WORD SAYS IF I DRAW NEAR TO YOU, YOU WILL DRAW NEAR TO ME. I WANT TO BE NEAR TO YOU. HELP US TO SEE CLEARLY WHEN WE CAN SET ASIDE TIME TO SPEND WITH YOU, AND HELP US NEVER TO COMPROMISE THAT TIME.

- IN JESUS NAME - AMEN

Devotion Day 5. The Vow of Preparation

Planning a wedding is one such milestone that couples invest in. The focus would appear to be in ensuring that the wedding day, ceremony and reception goes smoothly and that the honeymoon is planned in detail.

In contrast, most couples spend very little time planning for married life even though there are numerous things to consider. There are many things that can be done to begin preparing and building a lifelong and happy marriage. Investing in one's relationship and exploring each other's values, beliefs, customs and culture is essential. Couples who do so subsequently reap the rewards and enjoy the benefits for years to come.

God calls each of us to be better prepared for the one He has chosen for us. The vows of **Preparation, Priority, Pursuit, Partnership** and the vow of **Purity** is seen in the following couples. The first testimonies come from a couple named **Tyler** and **Beth**.

Tyler *and* ***Beth*** weren't prepared to meet each other via text message, however they were prepared for marriage. When they finally met face to face, the rest is history!

They share their story on **Preparation**:

Beth:
When two hearts combine, it's a beautiful thing, but it's not all pretty. A healthy relationship requires honesty, even about your baggage. My baggage held emotional scars from a previous marriage. My trust was wrecked and my fears were inflated like airbags. Still, in Isaiah 43:19, God told His people not to dwell on the past but to recognise that He's doing something new. I sensed that God had something new in store for me too. So, I decided to get intentional about preparing.

I prayed, I consistently read God's Word. I listened to wise friends. I saw a counsellor. I studied books about healing. I waited patiently on Gods timing.

Through it all, God used my negative experience and healing to reshape me. Then when my heart met Tyler's, we just fit. I love how He does that. Now, when the old fears try to creep back in, I have the trust to talk about them and the strength to fight them.

Tyler:
I've been praying for my future wife since I was a teenager. Over the years, I felt like God gave me specific words to focus on: 'intentionally' 'patience', and 'consistency'.

When I met Beth, I quickly knew she was the one I'd been praying for. She was always honest about how she was feeling and what she struggles with helped me be honest with her about my own pains from the past. We would constantly remind each other of the truth found in Psalm 147:3 that God heals the broken. As we dated, we lived out the three words God gave me. We loved each with intentionality, with patience, and consistency. It's incredible to recount how God prepared us not just for marriage, but for each other. Yeah, I got the girl I prayed for, but I keep praying because preparation doesn't end at the altar. I pray God will continue to prepare us and remake us for each new thing He does.

Jonathan and *Michelle* share their story on **Priority:**
This couple have been married for 10 years and feel they're at their best while serving others and laughing around the table with friends.

Jonathan:

'Thou shalt have no other Gods before me' (Exodus 20:3-5 NKJV)

Seems simple. I don't worship gods or other religions. Of course I don't bow down to a fictitious higher power or follow the teachings of other faiths. Check. I've got that commandment on lock. What does this have to do with my marriage? Says Jonathan.

Not so fast. Try reading it like this, *'have no other thing or no other person before me'*. Things I can easily put over Christ; my marriage, my job, my kids, my health, and more. All good things. Until they move God out of the top spot. Then they are gods. Here's what I realised: when the demands of life feel overwhelming, it's often because I've put something or somebody before God.

Putting nothing before Christ isn't easy, but it's for your good. When your priorities are in order – God first and marriage second – there's not just harmony, but there's deep peace, comfort, and spiritual confidence in you that can't be stopped.

Michelle:

Too often, I find myself realising I've accidentally replaced God as #1 and Jonathan as my #2 with other things simply by lacking clear priorities! I've even put my favourite hobbies first!

Putting God first means intentional time with Him, reading His Word, seeking Him first above everything. Everything! And it doesn't just effect me. When my priorities are wrong, my needs aren't met, and I end up looking to Jonathan to meet them. Basically, I ask him to put me first. That's simply not fair. Only God can fill my needs completely. Thankfully, I'm learning and relying on my marriage. It can only be strong as I am strong in the Lord. And putting God first is the only way that works.

Next, is a story of *Ryan* and *Ashia*, they are high school sweethearts who share their story on the topic of **Pursuit:**

Ryan:

The first thing I had to learn in marriage was that pursuit didn't end at the altar. I always told myself growing up that I'd never be a workaholic or who never spent time with his family. I didn't realise how easy it was to fall into that trap. Just weeks into our marriage, I had to learn to not bring home my work frustrations, to-do lists, or even the computer. I've started to pray on my way home for God's help to slow down and intentionally shift my mind and heart from my work to my wife. Confusing wife and work-just doesn't work. It's way too easy to tell yourself, '*My wife will always be here. I need to give more to work now so I can enjoy her later'*. What you treasure and pursue now is where you will end up later. Jesus taught us in Matthew 6:21 that where your treasure is found is the same place your heart is found. The vow of pursuit is about knowing where your treasure is and never giving up your search for it.

Ashia:

For Ryan and me, marriage brought with it a built-in accountability partner to keep our hearts pursuing God, always. We regularly challenge each other to grow our love and passion for God and His word. As a result, my desire to pursue Ryan increases. At the same time, I see his heart open with care and passion for me. This vow to pursue God, then each other, has made dating better and our marriage stronger.

Sounds perfect, right? Well, it's only taken a few months of marriage to realise we fall short of this deal. I find myself wanting to pursue Ryan by trying to meet all of his needs myself. Then I swing the opposite direction, trying to take care of only myself instead. This back and forth can be hurtful and endless until I remember our challenge to pursue God first. You see, when I pursue God, He in turn creates a desire in me to serve and pursue Ryan. When I trust God and Ryan, I find my needs are met. It's a side-by-side kind of pursuit. To paraphrase the Apostle Paul from Philippians 1:27 *'What ever happens, conduct yourselves in a manner worthy of the gospel of Christ'*. Ryan and I are standing firm in one spirit, with one mind striving side by side in our faith. How does all this pursuing work so well? Because God first pursued us.

Married 17 years, **Michael** and **Shelley** work together, play together, eat together, love together and parent three daughters together. They see marriage as a **Partnership** of one flesh but, it wasn't always that way.

Shelley:
Early in our marriage, I dreaded football season. Michael would want to enjoy a day of football while I saw Saturdays as 'honey do' day. After several football seasons of frustration, I decided to pray. I just wanted my husband to do the things I wanted to do (selfish, I know). God helped me with a thought

like this: *"Can you love what he loves?"* Saturday football became 'our' thing. Guess what happened next? Michael began pausing the game to help me with my projects. God helped me realise that I hadn't been treating my husband like a partner. In fact, I didn't even understand what partnership was. Today, our marriage is stronger than ever. We're one flesh – three strands that can't easily be broken. That is largely because we've learned to love each other by loving each other's passions.

Michael:

Shelly and I have been partners for a while, so it's easy to take her for granted. Sometimes I feel like I am the one doing all the work while she just coasts on my momentum. (I know, I know.) and when I do, I bet she feels the same way about me. Recently, Shelly went out of town for an entire week, and any notion that I was creating the momentum left with her. Just trying to style hair, pack lunches, make coffee, and get the kids on the bus things we do together everyday were overwhelming. It's been 17 years, and I'm still learning we have unique strengths in this partnership. Her strengths complement my weaknesses, and mine hers. We fit.

The two of us are becoming 'one flesh'. It's not that she compliments me. Only God does that. But with Him we're two complete individuals being forged in the fires of our passions and adversity into something totally new. Believe me, we are so much better together. Finally, Couples *James* and *Mandy* share their personal story on **Purity:** When James met Mandy, he knew she was the one. Mandy…not so much. But, years of friendship became a wonderful marriage. A year into marriage, they consider purity one of the most important commitments.

Mandy:

I grew up around church, so when I was a kid, all my friends talked about purity. Purity rings were the rage. I assumed purity was something about not giving your body to a boy. To me, that meant no kissing or anything else until marriage. I think a lot of people viewed purity this way, about not doing something physical. Since then, I've learned its way more than that. Purity is about your heart. When James and I were dating, instead of merely avoiding something, we chose to pursue Christ first. When you truly seek God with all your heart, He helps you remain pure. Now that we're married, we're still pure. But that doesn't mean we're abstaining! I'll never forget a moment of our honeymoon. Full of emotion, I realised how holy marriage really is. I looked at James, and said "I get it now, more than ever. Choosing purity was so worth it." So, even if you've made mistakes, you can still choose purity because purity is about pursuing Christ with all your heart. I promise you, it's worth it.

James:

Unlike Mandy, I didn't grow around church. Purity was a huge challenge. During my teenage years I developed an unhealthy view of women and a destructive relationship with pornography. After graduating high school, I gave my life to Christ. I knew I wanted to marry someone who pursued Jesus with everything they had. I also knew winning over a girl like that meant I needed to pursue Jesus with obedience. So, I changed my phone settings to only access websites I needed for work. Also, I had a close friend of mine regularly ask me how I was doing. My Pastor, put it well when he said *'Why resist a temptation tomorrow that you can eliminate today'?* A year into marriage, Mandy and I realise the vow of purity remains just as important today as it was before we ever met. And like Mandy said, it's worth it. These, are just a few testimonies which some of us can relate to when dating, or pursuing marriage. While these are important considerations for all couples, it's timely for couples planning to marry or commit to think and talk about these issues together.

DAY 5 Devotion Questions
The Vow of Preparation

Briefly describe how you are preparing the vows of **Preparation, Priority, Pursuit, Partnership** and the vow of **Purity** with your spouse. If you are already married, do these values still apply today?

1. Preparation

_____
_____
_____
_____

2. Priority

_____
_____
_____
_____

3. Pursuit

_____
_____
_____
_____

4. Partnership

_____
_____
_____
_____
_____

5. Purity

_____
_____
_____
_____
_____
_____

Pause and Pray

'LORD BLESS OUR MARRIAGE. TEACH US TO HONOUR YOU IN OUR FUTURE MARRIAGE BY RESPECTFULLY BLESSING AND SUPPORTING ONE ANOTHER. SHOW US WHAT HEALTHY MUTUAL HONOUR LOOKS LIKE, TAKING THE TIME TO LISTEN TO AND CONSIDER ONE ANOTHER. I'M PRAYING YOU WILL BLESS OUR MARRIAGE. MAY WE BE GRATEFUL FOR THE GIFT THAT IS OUR MARRIAGE'.

- IN JESUS NAME, AMEN.

Chapter Five

A Nautical View

'Christ did not die simply that you might be saved from a bad conscience, or even to remove the stain of past failure, but to "clear the decks" for divine action'.

– Ian Thomas

Devotion Day 1

One day Jesus said to his disciples, *'Let us go over to the other side of the lake'*. So they got into a boat and set out. As they sailed, he fell asleep. A squall came down on the lake, so that the boat was being swamped, and they were in great danger. The disciples went and woke him, saying, *'Master, Master, we're going to drown'*! He got up and rebuked the wind and the raging waters; the storm subsided, and all was calm. *'Where is your faith'*? he asked his disciples. In fear and amazement they asked one another, *'Who is this? He commands even the winds and the water, and they obey him'* (Luke 8:22-25 NIV).

We don't have to be those who put out to sea in boats to get the message. For each of us, the sea of family hardship, is threatening enough. Will we be overwhelmed by all this? Is it all too much? Do we have enough faith or strength to not only face but survive this all encompassing sea? The answer to that lies in the 'boat' we are in. It may seem small, but that doesn't mean it will capsize or sink. It may be tossed about and we may have a bout of seasickness as the storms swirl around us. But we can stay afloat. Sometimes we have to look back over our family circumstances in order to see where we came from and ask ourselves 'How did I get here'? 'Why is my life or marriage in trouble'? You may be sailing rough seas, but your 'boat' can still cling to God.

Our fragile yet real faith that somehow our God will get us through even if we don't know how. It is not so much the nature of our 'boat' that matters. It is *who* is in the boat with us.

Throughout the Bible, we find many stories involving boats. Looking at the disciples time with Jesus, we find many times that Jesus told them to get in the boat. Let's take a look at some of the benefits of getting in the boat. I grew up around boats, I have been on ferries and cruise ships, I enjoy the adrenaline and the smell of the open sea. My father owned a boat. We would often take the boat out on Lake Taupo (New Zealand) and fish for Rainbow Trout. We would glide across the open lake, it was smooth like ice. It was never fun when the lake was rough with a high swell. The boat would pound down on the waves, as he steered the boat back to shore. Life with Dad and his fishing boat was never dull. He would either forget to put the bung in, his hat would fly off, or not enough petrol. This didn't put me off boating. These life lessons taught me confidence and resilience as when the waves in life got rough I knew through faith, that the waters would soon become calm again.

Mark 6:31-32 reads, *'He said to them, 'Come away by yourselves to a remote place and rest for a while.' For many people were coming and going, and they did not even have time to eat. So they went away in the boat by themselves to a remote place,...'* How many times have you found yourself exhausted from work, ministry, parenting, or life in general. Although these are all good things, we have to find time to rest and rejuvenate to be able to carry on and be at our best. The boat provided this needed rest for the disciples.

What boat is the Lord giving you for rest? Get in the boat and receive your rest!. Mark 6:45 reads, *'Immediately He made His disciples get into the boat and go ahead of Him to the other side…'"…Immediately He spoke with them and said, 'Have courage! It is I. Don't be afraid.' Then He got into the boat with them, and the wind ceased. They were completely astounded',* Mark 6:50-51.

You're already in the boat! You're already on your way, going somewhere. Maybe you were obedient in starting a new job, or maybe you're on your way, building a family. Maybe you're working to provide for your family, or you're serving the local church, or you're pursuing building godly friendships in your life. You're figuratively in the boat, and you're on your way to the destination. Like the disciples, I think when we are on our way to a destination, we are focused on where we are headed. But here, Jesus reminds us of what is really important. It's not as much about where you're heading, but it's more about who is with you in the boat.

Although Jesus sent them out in the boat, they still experienced a storm and struggled. We can be right in the middle of God's Will and still face storms and struggles. The most important thing is to remain in His Will.

Devotional Questions Day 1
A Nautical View

Are you in the middle of a storm or struggle right now? In order to move forward from a storm, it is helpful to look back and understand how you got where you are. This family checkup will help you access and address the clutter that needs to be cleared from the decks of your marriage. Take a few moments to stop. Think back to your childhood. How would you describe the dynamics and atmosphere in your home? (For example: Peaceful, chaotic, loving, unloving, abusive, toxic, fearful, wonderful, warm, nurturing, cold or hostile).

_____
_____

In your own words, describe your parents. Your overall relationship with them. What was your communication, affection and friendship like?

_____
_____
_____

The things which bought joy into your life growing up and want to duplicate in your own home are... The things which bought sadness and don't want to repeat in your marriage and family are...

_____
_____
_____
_____
_____

Based on your answers, what do you and your spouse need to clear from the decks of your marriage?

_____
_____
_____
_____
_____

Pause and Pray

'LORD BLESS OUR MARRIAGE. THANK YOU THAT THIS STORM WILL NOT LAST FOREVER, BUT WE'RE ONLY PASSING THROUGH. YOU KNOW OUR JOURNEY BETTER THAN WE KNOW IT OURSELVES, AND YOU WILL USE THIS TIME OF TESTING FOR GOOD.

IN JESUS NAME - AMEN

Devotion Day 2. Equally Yoked

We'v all heard those big questions… 'Is it OK for Christians to online date'? and 'Are you really supposed to wait until you get married to have sex'? And of course, 'What does it mean to be equally yoked'? And why does it matter? The thing is, we don't hear a lot of practical dating advice about this in the church. If you're like me, you hear the same Bible verses repeated without any idea of what to do with them today. For example: 'unequally yoked'. What does that even mean? What does it look like to be unequally yoked? Why is it bad? And if it is so bad, how can you avoid it? The verse I'm talking about, and the verse I get so excited about, is 2 Corinthians 6:14. The NIV translation says, *'Do not be unequally yoked together with unbelievers. For what do righteousness and wickedness have in common? Or what fellowship can light have with darkness'?* The longer I've been married, the more I understand why it's important to be with someone who loves Jesus like I do. I truly believe that when Paul wrote the letter to the Corinthians, it was less like laying down the law and more like showing concern for a dear friend. He knew that when two people make a giant promise to stay together forever, they should have the same picture in their heads of what they want their life together to look like. A relationship lacking alignment in faith and values is destined to fail. I can remember the feeling of being in a relationship that just wasn't quite right for me. It felt like one of us was always compromising, like we weren't in step with each other's lives. Then one day I realised what was wrong: We weren't heading in the same direction. I wanted to be pursuing Jesus. I wanted to have His fingerprints all over my life. I had a clear direction, kind of like I was on a road headed straight North. Even though he voiced a different denomination, he believed pretty casually. He didn't want Jesus to be a big deal in his everyday life. It's like he was heading East. How would my story have ended with him? At best, we would have gone North-East, in a direction neither of us wanted to go. Now imagine you're heading towards your best life, including the relationship with Jesus that you want to have. And then you look to the side and see someone who is keeping pace with you, doing the same things. When you're walking in the same direction, you get to say, *'Hey, maybe we could do this together'!* You are connected spiritually, the same spirit - the same yoke. Both are heading True North!

The Bible warns against being unequally yoked in 2 Corinthians 6:14. Because the phrase *'unequally yoked'* can be a bit difficult to understand, I like to read this verse from The Message, a paraphrase of the Bible. These verses read, *'Don't become partners with those who reject God. How can you make a partnership out of right and wrong? That's not partnership; that's war. Is light best friends with dark?'* God gives us this command for our own protection and joy. He knows that we can't have the best possible marriage if we have different beliefs, values, and priorities from our spouse. And even though obedience to God can be difficult, especially in a situation like this, it's always worth it. Some Christians may find themselves saying, 'But this person will change'. Maybe so. God has the power to change someone, and we should never give up on praying for those we care about. However, the verse in 2 Corinthians doesn't say, 'Do not be unequally yoked ... unless you think the person will change'. It says, *'Do not be yoked together with unbelievers'*

Can you be unequally yoked with a church? A person can be unequally yoked with a church by being unequally matched in spiritual maturity, belief, or commitment, which can lead to a lack of shared purpose and spiritual struggle. This can occur with someone who identifies as a Christian but does not live a Christian lifestyle, or with someone who has conflicting core beliefs and values. It is important to look beyond a person's claims and examine their actions and heart to see if they are truly living a Christian lifestyle and growing in their faith.

Many people have experienced conflict within a church, often from those who have come from different denominations. Over time, their spirit struggles to connect with denominational differences, outworking of worship and discipleship. The outcome leads to frustration instead of peace within your spirit.

Why is being equally yoked so important? Equally yoked means you are of the same mind and heart in your faith walking with Jesus Christ. As Christians, it is important because being equally yoked allows you to grow and move together. Yes, there will be some seasons where one person may mature faster than the other, but the time period is usually short. Being equally yoked, spiritually, is wonderful when both couples know how to come to God together in prayer, worship and unity. This is known as being 'equally yoked'.

Devotional Questions Day 2

Equally Yoked

A yoke is a wooden bar or frame by which two animals, like oxen, are joined at the heads or necks for working together. The yoke is designed to equip oxen to carry a load. Two oxen yoked together can carry such a load more effectively than one alone, because the yoke enables the weight to be distributed between the two. The oxen works together to carry things in service to their master. When we work alongside others and bear one another's burdens, we're yoking ourselves together with them. As we work toward similar ends and share each other's struggles, we form close relationships. Did you know that two draft horses can pull three times as much weight as one alone? And if those horses are trained together from the beginning, they can pull up to four times as much as one alone. I suspect there are two main reasons for this:

1. They've developed a relationship
2. They have the same master and trainer

Our master, is God. When we're yoked together with other Christians, we have a shared goal to serve Christ and we're working from the same training manual: The Bible. This already gives us a great starting point. When we have similar upbringings and worldviews, this makes it even easier for us to work together.

Can a Christian be equally yoked to a non-Christian?

_____
_____
_____
_____

What Does Equally Yoked Mean? Where Did the Term Yoke Come From?

_____
_____
_____
_____

Why Is It Important to Be Equally Yoked in Dating or in Marriage?

_____
_____
_____
_____

Devotion Day 3. Christs Coordinates

The captain of the ship is the one who navigates the ship and keeps it on course. In the home, while the husband is responsible to chart and map the course of the new home, he is not able, of himself to always make wise decisions. No one has all the wisdom and insights to see ahead far enough to negotiate the dangers that are unforeseeable. Just as it would be insane to begin a journey across the desert without a guide, so it would be to cross the ocean without a compass. This can also be said for of marriage. Ships do not empower themselves. They need an engine. Neither do marriages thrive on their own steam. Good marriages are not the result of fate, or chance, or good luck. There is planning, purpose, and divine intent.

Ships need anchors. Anchors keep them from drifting while resting in the harbour. The anchor of successful marriages is simply the old time traditional values. The commitment to love and cherish your spouse 'in sickness and health, richer or poorer until death do you part' is of greatest importance. The promise to love and cherish is unconditional. With such resolve, a Captain who knows the way, and the Holy Spirit to guide you, no storm can sink your ship. Ships also need provisions for the journey. So do marriages.

'*Mooring*' is a nautical term, that refers to an anchor to which a ship is secured to prevent it from being carried away by waves. Gods design for marriage is flawless and somewhat similar as being the anchor to our souls. I've been on many boats, and the largest have been cruise ships. See, once you've made the decision to climb aboard a cruise ship, there is nothing left to do but enjoy the benefits of your well-planned vacation. But, I'll admit, the first cruising experience was less than perfect. This bad experience however, hasn't spoiled my view from getting on the next ship. Doesn't that remind you of relationSHIPS? We don't give up on our relationSHIPS because of one bad experience or memories from past 'ships'.

How many of you are jumping ship eager to seek a divorce every time your journey becomes less than perfect according to your standards, values or demands? Why do we wait until we are navigating our ship that is desperately off track with ripped sails, lost/damaged cargo, and frayed ropes, instead of soundly positioning ourselves with Jesus to make a way. Staying with the nautical theme, no one wants to trip or sink.

Have you ever heard the phrase True North? True North is a concept of the lean management process that works as a compass to guide an organisation from the current conditions to where it wants to reach. It acts as a mission statement that reflects the purpose of the organisation and the foundation of a strategic plan.

So, to find our true north, we discover our authentic selves; that is the bottom line. It is a combination of our purpose and our beliefs. We decide what we value most in life and put that to the forefront. Once we know this inner sense, we are one step closer to answering our calling. Our true north is unique to us as individuals. According to Mark, the True North that the whole world depends on to be reconciled back to God is Jesus Christ. The very first part of Mark says what his entire letter is about. Jesus is our True North. We need to remind ourselves of this daily and sometimes hourly.

Our true north is Jesus. When we are in uncertain situations, how much we can tolerate and navigate uncertainty will have a lot to do with how much truth we have hidden and how much truth we know. How much trust we have depends on how much truth we have hidden.

If you are having a hard time trusting God in the area of your marriage right now, it may be a sign that you have not hidden the truth in your hearts deeply enough for that situation to be resolved. When we have a good sense of where we are going, we can be in strange situations but still have a profound, solid understanding of faith. If we believe we are no one or have no one, those beliefs will keep us stuck in a view of insignificance or isolation.

A lot of times, we think God will get us out of a situation if we didn't get ourselves into them. We do dumb stuff and need God to deliver us from our own hands and decisions.

God doesn't waste any words. What He says comes to pass. He is there for everyone, not just us. We expect people to be happy when God does something in our lives. What if they aren't? Does that matter? When God blesses us, we should be humble; when we see Him bless others, we should thank God.

I want to encourage you today that God's path for your life will always lead you into a full and abundant life. God really wants to be the captain of your relationship, so let us choose to put our hand into the hand of Jesus and follow His voice and promptings. You can follow His direction because when you make Jesus your compass you marriage will never get lost.

Devotional Questions Day 3
Christ's Coordinates

The captain of the ship is the one who navigates the ship and keeps it on course. In the home, while the husband is responsible to chart and map the course of the home, he is not able, of himself to always make wise decisions. No one has all the wisdom and insights to see ahead far enough to negotiate the dangers that are unforeseeable.

Discussion Questions

Many married couples live in survival mode. However God doesn't want marriages that barely survive. He wants marriages to thrive! Take a few moments to share any dangers or possible 'red flags'. What do they look like?

_____
_____
_____
_____

Many times our fears in the present are birthed out of disappointments, hurts, and feeling on being unloved from the past. Afraid of being hurt again. We unknowingly attempt to make our spouse pay the price for our behaviours. For example; verbal put downs, belittlement, isolation, narcissist personality disorder, gas lighting, silence, stonewalling, jealousy, intensity and volatility. These are toxic and cripple relationships.

Discuss any experiences you may of had. How did you handle the situation? Where was God during your storm. How did God navigate your life back to Him?

_____
_____
_____
_____
_____
_____

Pause and Pray

'LORD BLESS OUR MARRIAGE'. HOW CAN I TRUST YOU MORE AND SEE THESE AREAS OF MY LIFE DISSOLVE FROM MY LIFE? BE STILL AND LISTEN. WHAT IS GOD REVEALING?
IN JESUS NAME - AMEN.

Devotion Day 4. Below the water level

There is something special about being out on a lake in a sail boat. There is a simple quietness that can be felt as you glide through the water, free from the overwhelming growl of a noisy motor. There is a peaceful joy that takes over as you feel the warm sun and cool breeze blending on your face in perfect harmony. If you have ever been out on a sail boat, you know exactly what I am taking about. It is what is below the water line that determines the readiness of a sail boat to withstand a storm. Below a sail vessel, there is something called a 'keel' and a 'ballast'. The keel is what allows the captain to steer the boat and stay on course and not be tossed and turned by the wind and waves. The ballast is a heavy weight strategically placed on the bottom of the keel. This off setting weight exists to keep the boat upright and prevent it from being capsized in extreme conditions.

As followers of our Lord and Saviour, we are called to be prepared in order to stay upright and on course in the wind and waves of the storms we encounter in this world. In Colossians 2 and Philippians 4, the Apostle Paul gives us instructions on what we need to possess below our spiritual waterline to ready ourselves for any and all situations. Colossians 2:6-7 reads,

> *'So then, just as you received Christ Jesus as Lord, continue to live your lives in him, rooted and built up in him, strengthened in the faith as you were taught, and overflowing with thankfulness'.* Philippians 4:6-7 *'Do not be anxious about anything, but in every situation, by prayer and petition, with thanksgiving, present your requests to God. And the peace of God, which transcends all understanding, will guard your hearts and your minds in Christ Jesus'.*

Being rooted in our faith in Jesus Christ and in his word is like the keel in our lives that keeps us from being blown back and forth by the winds of hardship and the waves of sin we face each day. God's word gives us the strength and guidance that is required to face our earthly struggles head on. When the bystanders of the world observe the life of a Christian, it is often only what is above the water line that they are able to witness. In our brokenness of pain, and uncertainty, what is below the water line becomes exposed. In these times, the strength of being rooted in the keel of God's word and the untippable power of being grounded in the ballast of prayer creates a remarkable combination. A combination that can withstand even the most powerful of storms and one that will surely be noticed by others. Our witness to those around us during a crisis will surely be marked by our dependence on these two essentials. Being in an unhealthy relationship can tip your sails and put both of you off course. Maybe this is your storm today. Maybe now would be a good time to take a look at what is below your spiritual water line.

Have you ever experienced days where feel like you're sinking below the water level? You find yourself searching for faith. God knows every marriage will have these moments. He gave us help in His Word to encourage couples when weakness threatens the trust we have in Him. Great men and women throughout history had times when their faith decreased. And from their stories, we can find the help we need to restore ours.

Historians will probably call our era 'the age of anxiety', Anxiety is the natural result when our hopes are centered in anything short of God and His will for us. When we make anything else our goal, frustration and defeat are inevitable. Though we have less to worry about than previous generations, we have more worry. Though we have it easier than our forefathers, we have more uneasiness. Though we have less real cause for anxiety than our predecessors. Couples today are inwardly more anxious. Society is going in one direction, and the a Christian marriage is going in the opposite direction. This brings about friction and conflict. As we anchor our hope in God, our perspective shifts. We begin to see beyond our present circumstances, and we focus on the unchanging nature of our heavenly Father. He is the source of true joy and peace, and in Him we find strength to persevere.

Our weakness in faith reminds us to renew our trust in God's strength.

- *For you said, I am your chosen child.*
- *For you said, you will never leave me.*
- *For you said, you will guide and protect me.*

God's Word promises, *'My grace is sufficient for you, for My strength is made perfect in weakness'.* (2 Corinthians 12:9). So we can rely on His strength even more when our faith is weak. Let's remind ourselves of His unfailing love today by starting with these three words.

For you said...

Devotional Questions Day 4
Below the Water Level

Most of us have experienced some form of pain from the choices we have made in our lives. Sexual choices, addictions, abuse, unhealthy relationships. God made a way to heal and restore our lives through His Son, Jesus.

Are there experiences from your past, or your spouses past, that make either of you feel like you don't deserve one another? Take a few moments to be still. Allow the Holy Spirit to speak to your heart, write down and surrender it to God in prayer. Get together with your group and share your heart on this issue with each other. Pray and invite the Holy Spirit to heal your heart and restore whats been lost.

_____

_____

_____

_____

_____

How is your keel of faith? Are you being strengthened by spending time each day in God's word and applying it to your life? Or are you crippled with hurt? How is your ballast of prayer? Are you connecting daily to the one who is the giver and sustainer of life?

_____
_____
_____
_____
_____
_____
_____
_____
_____
_____

PAUSE AND PRAY

'LORD BLESS OUR MARRIAGE'. WE COME TO YOU WITH TROUBLES THAT ARE WEIGHING ON OUR HEARTS. GOD, WE KNOW THAT YOU CARRY ALL BURDENS, AND WE ASK THAT YOU SHARE YOUR YOKE WITH US NOW DURING THIS DIFFICULT TIME.

IN JESUS NAME - AMEN

DEVOTION DAY 5. HOPE AFTER THE STORM

When it comes to learning how to love yourself, experiencing a loving relationship with another person has the potential to be profoundly healing. Healthy relationships have the ability to encourage self-love. But when you've lived through a toxic relationship, you also know the dark side of relationships, which is that they can also be terribly destructive to your self-esteem and sense of self-worth. Learning to love yourself *just as you are* is a vital part of healing after a breakup, especially when the relationship was toxic or abusive. Healing after a toxic relationship begins with healing your relationship with yourself and rediscovering your innate self-worth. One of the things that can make letting go of a toxic relationship so difficult is that healing requires you come to terms with how you were treated in the relationship. When I work with individuals healing from past relationships, one of the first questions they ask is, '*How did I let this happen to me? What's wrong with me'?* So, let's get something straight before we go any further. Nothing's wrong with you. Bad things happen to good people.

We can *all* end up in unhealthy relationships where we allow ourselves to be treated poorly, especially because until you've been in a toxic relationship, it's nearly impossible to see it coming. When you look back on the relationship after it's over, it's so much easier to see all the signs of a toxic relationship that you couldn't see when you were still in the midst of the relationship. It's vital to be gentle with yourself as you start looking back at the relationship, so that you don't spiral into shame and self-judgment about what you tolerated in the relationship. I've guided many people through the process of healing from toxic relationships.

The first part of recovery almost always involves working through feelings of embarrassment, shame or guilt about how bad the relationship was. The rest is up to you and God.

A hail storm can knock down flowers and, sometimes, God knocks us to our knees with a storm of troubles. It's when we're on our knees, however, that the only place to look is up! When we ask God to reveal Himself to us, we shouldn't expect Him to do it with a job or financial support. After all, God only promises relief from *all* of our troubles in the next world. In this life, we will be relieved only from *some* of them; other troubles He will enable us to endure. Nevertheless, when we humbly and sincerely ask God to reveal himself to us, He will. If God seems far away, who moved? The storms in marriage often come without warning. These are situations that disturb us physically, financially, or emotionally. And because storms vary in type and intensity, they test our faith in different ways. Sometimes, in the middle of a strong storm, we might even wonder if we'll make it through. But just because your faith is struggling doesn't mean it will crash. So, how can you know for sure that you'll still be standing after the storm?

First, realise that storms are inevitable. You're either in one right now, coming out of one, or about to enter one. Troubles don't vanish just because you're a Christian. In fact, they might actually increase. Jesus said, 'we must go many warships to enter the kingdom of God' (Acts 14:22). He knew we'd experience the hardships of living in a fallen world, plus the adversity of living out our faith. Storms also test whether you really believe what you say you believe. The Bible speaks of those who claim faith but don't cling to it. For example, Peter and Judas faced the same storm, the arrest and death of Jesus, but the results were entirely different. Both men stumbled, either denying or betraying Jesus. While Peter trusted Jesus enough to recover, Judas' foundation was revealed as false faith. One storm—two results. Stumbling faith doesn't have to be crashing faith. Genuine faith in Jesus Christ eventually weathers the storm. That's why you need to check your foundation; because storms test your faith and reveal what kind of foundation you have. If your faith is built on peace and prosperity, you'll be overcome when a strong storm hits your relationship. What is your present storm revealing about your faith? Are you stumbling and struggling? That's okay. Remember, faith that cannot be tested cannot be trusted. God already knows every difficulty you will ever face. Your current circumstances haven't caught Him off guard. Are you trusting Christ as your firm foundation?

Then cling to Him in the midst of the storm, and you'll still be standing after the storm passes by.

'Lord, help'! they cried in their trouble, and he saved them from their distress. He calmed the storm to a whisper and stilled the waves. What a blessing was that stillness as he brought them safely into harbor! (Psalm 107:28-30 NLT)

Devotional Questions Day 5

Hope after the Storm

Bad relationships gradually erode your sense of self-worth. In a toxic relationship, your sense of what a healthy relationship looks like gets confused and distorted over time.

Once your perception of what's normal gets distorted, You're not able to see the signs of an unhealthy relationship that would have stood out like a neon sign at the beginning of the relationship. One of the things that can make letting go of a toxic relationship so difficult is that you have to come to terms with how you were treated in the relationship. This is often a slow, confusing, and painful process.

Are you able to let go of the unhealthy relationship?

_____
_____
_____
_____
_____

Ask yourself, how did this happen to me? Are you learning to trust yourself? As well as your sense of reality.

_____
_____
_____

Who are you blaming? Are you allowing yourself to grieve? Where is God in your grief?

_____
_____
_____

What steps are you taking in order to move forward and feel good?

_____
_____
_____

PAUSE AND PRAY

'LORD BLESS OUR MARRIAGE'. I TURN TO YOU FOR HOPE. YOU ARE THE SOURCE OF ALL HOPE AND THE LIGHT THAT SHINES IN THE DARKNESS. LORD, HELP ME TO TRUST IN YOUR PLAN.

IN JESUS NAME - AMEN

Chapter six
Top Secret

Christ did not die simply that you might be saved from a bad conscience, or even to remove the stain of past failure, but to 'clear the decks' for divine action.

– Ian Thomas

Devotion Day 1

To understand the secret of serving one another within a marriage, we need to re-visit the Garden of Eden. Genesis 1:27 reminds us that '*God created human beings in His own image. In image of God He created them; male and female He created them*'. Both men and women are image-bearers reflecting the mirror image of God. Male and female have their differences, yet they are equally important in revealing the nature of God on this earth. Husband and wives are unique *roles*. The Bible points out specific details of what they entail, however these *roles* are not our identity. Our identities have to do with our original design. We were created as carriers of God's likeness on this earth. Although the 'fall' in Genesis 3, distorted this purpose, the sacrifice of Jesus restored it. Our salvation in Jesus is first and foremost a change of identity. There is no role - husband, wife, teacher, parent, or friend that can out rank your identity.

Because a change in role - single to being marriage, dissolves yourself of your former self, and be constantly renewed in the spirit on your mind, thus, having a fresh mindset and spiritual attitude, and put on a new nature, thus, regenerate self, created in God's image (Godlike), in true righteousness and Holiness. Ephesians 4:22-24 AMP reads; ' *that, regarding your previous way of life, you put off your old self (completely discard your former nature), which is being corrupted through deceitful desires, and be continually renewed in the spirit of your mind (having a fresh, untarnished mental and spiritual attitude), and put on a new self (the regenerated and renewed nature), created in Gods image, (godlike) in the righteousness and holiness of the truth in the way the expresses to God your gratitude for your salvation.*

Trying to love and serve God without the Spirit is like trying to water your garden with the fossil being connected to the water outlet. A hose can produce water on its own, you just have to turn on the tap…right? Likewise, its only when we fully embrace the empowerment of the Holy Spirit can we love and serve our spouse the way God desires.

My love language is acts of service. I feel loved and cared for when someone does something for me. My husband helps with unloading the dishwasher, grocery shopping, and other odd jobs around our home. Managing my home with a family and pets means endless tasks of serving. I love keeping a home, but sometimes, I feel unloved when no one is serving me. I want someone to notice something and do it for me. We each have our daily chores, which is fair.

We share nightly kitchen cleanup and Saturday house cleaning. But still, I long for someone to serve me.

Imagine my shock when my husband offers me breakfast or dinner in bed. I am always filled with delight. When My husband serves breakfast, I'm not talking plain cereal or a piece of toast. He has perfected breakfast making. In fact he is now our main cook in the kitchen. He prepares food of every kind from breakfast, lunch and dinner. Eggs Benedict, Sandwiches and wraps, fancy avocado on toast, roasted tomatoes, poached eggs and there's always herbs. He's constantly looking for new fanciful ideas. All this from a man who rarely cooked. He can flip a pancake and make a delicate dessert. This is his extravagant gift of service, and I feel cared for. What a simple gesture to fill my love tank. When I'm offered to rest up in bed and I'm served dinner in bed, I feel loved and cared for.

What an impact. We process our workdays together. We serve each other well in these moments as we create emotional intimacy through conversation.

Why serve?

We serve because Christ first served us (Matthew 20:28). When we roll up our sleeves, we mirror God's love to a world that desperately needs it. Serving can meet physical, emotional, and spiritual needs. Think about Jesus feeding the 5,000 (John 6:1–14). Those people were hungry, and Jesus didn't just preach; He fed them.

Your service might look like filling backpacks with school supplies, praying with someone who's hurting, or just showing up to visit a lonely neighbour. These small acts of kindness make a big impact.. They tell people, '*You matter. You are loved'*. Let's not forget, our actions can point others toward Jesus, your ultimate Servant.

Devotional Questions Day 1
Top Secret

Your growth is largely dependent on your ability to serve in a Christlike manner. Serving one-another is not always easy, and is rarely convenient. Serving pulls us out of ourselves and helps us focus on the needs of others. Yet for all that change in focus, it is that very service to others that teaches us the most about ourselves and how to greater appreciate what the Savior has done for us.

Reflect on the time you starting serving God. In what specific ways has the Holy Spirit transformed you for the better? How has He transformed your marriage?

_____
_____
_____
_____
_____
_____
_____
_____

As you go through your day of serving your spouse and family, can you identify times when it would be helpful if you put down your phone and looked at them instead? What is your behaviour and actions saying?

_____
_____
_____

What is the difference in how we connect with others when we are looking into their eyes as they talk, vs. only seeing text on a screen? Where is the value of this connection when serving someone?

_____
_____
_____

What are some of the differences between serving a stranger and serving a family member or a neighbour? Is there a difference in the quality of service one usually has to provide to a family member that may not be required in order to serve a stranger?

_____
_____
_____

Devotion Day 2. Honour your wife

In the beginning, God mentions it was not good for man to be alone. This was the first problem - man's isolation, the solution was to create Eve. Women are God's answers, not secondary creations. As you are a man of God, you have been entrusted with the opportunity to love, support, invest in and to serve your wife as a bold declaration of God's heart to the whole world that has crippled under the lies of the enemy. Peter continues by saying, That men are to treat their wives with understanding. Men are to seek and understand those who are different from themselves. All men are different and all women are different, and therefore men and women are different. My husband does not dishonour because I'm different from him, and I don't dishonour my husband because he is different from me. We would be notoriously boring if we were exactly the same. There have been occasions where our differences have clashed, yet through the hardship and weakness this has caused, it has opened the opportunity for our challenges to be exposed and strengthened.

How can a husband honour his wife?

1. Speak to her kindly.
2. Do not discuss her weaknesses with others.
3. Show interest in her projects.
4. Speak highly of her to your children.
5. Learn her likes and dislikes.
6. Learn her joys and sorrows.
7. Do not demean her health situations.
8. Remember her special days.
9. Do not treat her as a servant.
10. Do not compare her to other women.

These are simple thoughts, and you could add more. But start somewhere! I believe that if you invest honour into your wife, she'll give it back. It may not be tomorrow. But the process will strengthen your marriage. Remember, your wife is the person who you asked to marry you. And when you married, God made the two of you one flesh. Don't unravel, by neglect or criticism, what God has put together.

Honour your wife…so long as you both shall live.

The Bible reads; 1 Peter 3:7 *'Husbands, in the same way live with your wives, and treat them with respect as the weaker partner and as heirs with you of the gracious gift of life, so that nothing will hinder your prayers'.*

'Live with your wives' - This speaks about physically living in the same house as my wife.
- Am I spending regular, focused time with her?
- Do I understand her schedule and life?
- Am I mindful of her exhaustion limits?
- Am I eagerly sharing my load of the chores?
- **'An Understanding Way'** - This speaks about knowing my wife well, intellectually.
- Do I know the things that my wife likes/dislikes?
- Am I engaging her in meaningful conversation?
- Do I take an interest in what interests her?
- Do I ask her about what she's thinking on lately?

'Showing Honour to the Woman' - This speaks about looking out for your wife's emotional needs.
- What have I done lately to make my wife feel special?
- How am I encouraging her dreams and aspirations?
- Am I engaging in non-sexual love and affirmation?
- Am I making it possible for her to 'unwind'?

'So that your prayers may not be hindered' - This speaks about encouraging your wife spiritually.

• Are we praying through issues together?

• Am I setting a good example through my walk with God?

• Are we serving together in an area of our church?

To cherish your wife is to have a certain mindset or attitude toward her. Cherish means that you recognise your wife's incredible value. And even in those moments when you forget how valuable she is, her value never changes. Look at how God sees your wife:

- 'fearfully and wonderfully made'. (Psalm 139:14)
- 'treasured possession'. (Exodus 19:5)
- 'glorious inheritance'. (Ephesians 1:18)
- 'precious' (Isaiah 43:4)
- 'masterpiece...' (Ephesians 2:10)

These verses are dripping with worth and value, they show the essence of the word *cherish*. What's Your Plan? The plan here men, is not to make excuses; it's to realise you all need forward progress in these areas. And you are willing to make changes in your patterns to demonstrate greater honour towards your wife. Men, be encouraged to act like a gentleman toward your wife, demonstrate to her that she is your most valued blessing from God, and honour her with great respect. Doing so will pay high dividends here and in eternity.

Devotional Questions Day 2

Honour your wife

Men and woman are equal in marriage. The wife is not secondary to her husband, nor is the husband secondary to his wife. The two spouses are coheirs and have equal shares in the grace of God. How can you and your spouse best honour each other as equals? By learning and living out your God given role.

What is the Holy Spirit showing you about the role of the husband? The role of the wife?

_____
_____
_____
_____

Be honest, are you honouring your spouse by living out your God-given role? Write down any areas you feel you need to grow.

_____
_____
_____
_____

To honour your husband, ask him what makes him feel valued. Reflect on how your words and actions demonstrate respect, and consider how your spiritual walk with God impacts your marriage.

_____
_____
_____
_____

To honour your wife, ask her what makes her feel valued. Reflect on how your words and actions demonstrate respect, and consider how your spiritual walk with God impacts your marriage.

_____
_____
_____
_____

Pause and Pray

'LORD BLESS OUR MARRIAGE. HOLY SPIRIT SEARCH OUR HEART. WHAT IS KEEPING US FROM HONOURING EACH OTHER? WHAT ARE WE MISSING? PLEASE HELP US BOTH FIND OUR EXTRAORDINARY VALUE IN EACH OTHER'. IN JESUS NAME - AMEN

Devotion Day 3. Support your husband

Ephesians 5:22-24 reads: *'Wives, submit yourselves to your own husbands as you do to the Lord. For the husband is the head of the wife as Christ is the head of the church, his body, of which he is the Savior. Now as the church submits to Christ, so also wives should submit to their husbands in everything'*.

You'll recall Paul's instructions to husbands and wives by telling them to 'submit to one another for the reverence for Christ' (Ephesians 5:21). In the next verse, Paul elaborates *'For wives, this means submit to your husbands as to the Lord'*. Many misunderstand this verse and see it as a loss for women, but is not saying that. Remember marriage is not about domination, the wife shares in the exercise of being an equal partner. This does override the husbands role as headship of the house, for both husband and wife have unique areas of authority and influence within the marriage and in the world around them. The wife's support to her husband is an act of service. Wives you have been entrusted with the heart of your husband. Protecting his heart by speaking the truth with love and respect can be one of your greatest acts of service. Learn to serve him by helping express his heart. Rather than jumping to conclusions, help in grow in vision, purpose and strength. Enhance his life with effective communication. Woman are vulnerable in the area of physical strength. Whilst women are 'life bearers', woman are caretakers of mens hearts, just as men should be the protectors and providers for any physical weakness in their wives. As the husband initiates service and lays down his life for his wife, she responds by honouring him as the head of the union. This is her part in revealing the love of Christ to the world. Her honour, love and respect for her husband show what its like to be led by Jesus. God had not asked for women to submit because they are secondary. God is inviting them to display what the church should look like when led by a good, faithful and generous Lord and Savior. The world has become crippled as we have allowed these roles to be despised. In giving this role to women, God has asked his daughters to demonstrate that He is trustworthy.

God made women to be strong and capable. Throughout historic times, He has chosen women to lead, judge, prophesy, intercede and even bear and nurture His only begotten Son. In calling woman to respect the hardship of their husbands, He is not communicating that they are weak or unworthy. Instead,

God is revealing, 'I know you are capable and strong because you are *My* daughter. But in the eternal imagery of marriage, I need someone to show the goodness that is found in submission to Me. Will you willingly enter into the role of support and submission as a way of showing others I am deserving of devotion'? How can I encourage my husband to lead our family spiritually? How can I motivate my husband to read his Bible/pray with me/lead family devotions/serve in the church, or be a better role model in the workplace?. Most of us want our husbands to be the spiritual leaders in our home, to read the Bible with us, pray with us and for us, and guide our children in the ways of God. Sadly, few Christian men do this. Even fewer do it well. In many Christian homes the woman are more spiritually mature than the man. She reads and studies her Bible, initiates family devotions, and leads in prayer.

If this describes your situation, take heart. God is at work in your family. He can and will use you to influence them for Christ. You are not alone. I wish I could give you three steps to transform your husband into a dynamic spiritual leader who will shepherd his family well, love you as Christ loves the church, and impact God's kingdom.

I can't.

However, I can offer five suggestions to help you come alongside God as He works in and through your husband.

1. Pray.
2. Cultivate your relationship with God.
3. Look for creative ways to spend time with God together.
4. Ask your husband how you can pray for him, and ask him to pray for you,
5. Trust God's timing

When a man is discouraged, he is often down on himself most of all. So this would be the perfect time to affirm the good you can see in your husband that he might not be able to see for himself. Express your appreciation for the everyday tasks he does for you, and remind him of those unique qualities you love about him. Instead of pointing out what he isn't doing well, point out any positives, no matter how small. No matter what the circumstances, show him that he's No.1 in your life. Communicate that it's HIM; not his job, not his situation, not his wealth, but HIM that matters to you.

When life is overwhelming and you're struggling to find your way, remember that if everything else were gone tomorrow, your spouse is what truly matters.

Devotional Questions Day 3
Support your husband

Deepening your relationship requires real, concerted effort in order to learn about each other, to support and to grow together. Think about the role of the husband; to lead his wife by serving her as Jesus serves. In marriage, He provides a picture of the leadership service, and love of Jesus. Men, what motivates you in this role? What makes you feel insecure or uncertain?

_____
_____
_____
_____
_____

What social issue do you care about the most? Why?

_____
_____
_____
_____
_____
_____
_____

Where do you see yourself in the next 5, 10, or 20 years? Describe your perfect life at 65+.

_____
_____
_____
_____

If you could pick three of your character traits to pass on, what would you choose?

_____
_____
_____
_____

Pause and Pray

'LORD BLESS OUR MARRIAGE. THANK YOU FOR MY HUSBAND AND FOR THE GIFT HE IS TO MY LIFE. THANK YOU THAT HE IS A MAN OF INTEGRITY AND THAT OUR ENTIRE FAMILY IS BLESSED TO HAVE HIM AS OUR LEADER. I PRAY THAT HE FOLLOWS YOUR COMMAND TO LOVE YOU WITH ALL HIS HEART, ALL HIS SOUL, ALL HIS STRENGTH AND ALL HIS MIND.

IN JESUS NAME - AMEN

Devotion Day 4. Head Servant

Again, the role of a man is not one of domination. Dominating is different to leading. Leading requires dignity and choice, whilst dominating demands without options. According to the word of God, Jesus Christ is the head of the church. He is the head of every man and every woman. On earth, and in the family, He has set the husband as the head of the wife and therefore the head of the family. What does it mean to be the head of your house? If you desire to please God, then it certainly does not mean that you lord it over your family or boss them around, neither does it mean that you get to control them.

Jesus washed his disciples, feet and told them that their job was to love and serve others, just as He had loved and served them. Jesus laid down His very life for us and He asks us to do the same for others. Why would we serve others and not our own family? The husband is head of the wife, just as Jesus is Head of the church. Jesus put us ahead of Himself. He considered our need as greater than His own. Ephesians 5:25 reads *'husbands to love their wives, as Christ loved the church and gave Himself up for her'*. How does Jesus love His Church? That's how you should love and treat your wife. The word for love here is *agape,* the God-kind of love, not mere human love, but God's love. The love that sees others as valuable and precious, the love that can love sinners, the love that can love the unlovable! Not a conditional love, but rather an unconditional love.

The Hebrew word for 'head' means captain or chief. Husband, you are the captain of your own ship, being your family. The direction your family goes in is in your hands. Joshua declared, *'As for me and my house, we will serve the Lord'* (Joshua 24:15). The first and most important thing you need to do is to serve God with all your heart, soul, mind and strength, yourself, and to teach your children to do the same. They will follow and serve God if they know how much He loves them. You teach them how much God loves them, by loving and nurturing them yourself. This is good advice for every husband, not just ministers. If you are a minister, remember that your ministry is only as strong as your marriage. Husbands, your first priority is to love God with all your heart; your second priority is to love your wife with all your heart; your third priority is your children; your fourth is your career or your ministry. A man who has his priorities in order, and who obeys God's word regarding his wife and family, will have the fruit of a beautiful loving family, who serve the Lord together with him. *Praise the Lord! Blessed is the man who fears the Lord, Who delights greatly in His commandments. His descendants will be mighty on earth; The generation of the upright will be blessed. Wealth and riches will be in his house, And his righteousness endures forever,* (Psalms 112:1-3 NKJV).

What Is Servant Leadership? - Headship means assuming responsibility. Your wife, who is to be submissive to you, has every right to look to you to meet the needs she has as a wife in the home. This is not a chain of command; it is a line of responsibility. *'But I want you to know that the head of every man is Christ, the head of woman is man, and the head of Christ is God'* (1 Corinthians 11:3). God the Father and God the Son are equal. Yet the Bible says, *'The head of Christ is God'*. The submission of Jesus to the Father is not out of fear, but is based in love, because of love. So it is in the home. A home needs a head, and the Bible says that the head is the husband. There must be authority. 'Mutual submission' is not submission at all. In the home, the responsibility is on the husband. You cannot ignore it. No man can be the head of his home until he is under the headship of Christ. If he is not willing to be under Christ, what right does he have to the anointing power of God, to be the Godly husband God wants him to be? The husband is the one who is ultimately responsible for his children. Too many men are assuming that the mother is the one who is primarily responsible for raising the children. But no, it is you, the father, who must lead your children. Until recent times the majority of books on parenting were targeted not at mothers but at fathers. In the past people have understood what today we tend to ignore. Dad is primarily responsible for raising the children. If you do not lead your family, someone else will; someone else will have to. But God has called you to lead, to lead with great joy and delight, to lead though it may be costly, and to lead with love. Lead your wife, lead your family, and do it all for the glory of God. So, protect your wife and family, physically. Satan cannot get your family unless he comes through you. You are the head, the doorkeeper. Stand at your place, where God has put you.

'*I don't have what it takes*'. It's good that you recognise that. As you assume your responsibility, you have to be under the One who has assumed His responsibility to take care of you.

Devotional Questions Day 4
Head Servant

Talk about your responses to the following questions with your spouse; discuss your vision of what serving each other looks like within your marriage. Address any concerns or necessary adjustments.

Men, what excites you about the role of your wife? How can you honour your wife's role to bring about oneness into your marriage?

_____
_____
_____
_____
_____
_____
_____
_____
_____
_____
_____
_____
_____

Women, what excites you about the role of your husband? How can you honour your husbands role to bring about oneness into your marriage?

_____
_____
_____
_____
_____
_____
_____
_____
_____
_____

Pause and Pray

'LORD BLESS OUR MARRIAGE. WE THANK YOU THAT YOU HAVE HONOURED EACH OF US WITH A FLOURISHING, NOBLE AND WEIGHTY ROLE IN OUR MARRIAGE. LORD, PLEASE HELP US TO SERVE EACH OTHER AND TO BE OF INFLUENCE TO MODEL 'ONENESS' AND LOVE WELL, FOR YOUR GLORY IN HEAVEN ABOVE'.

IN JESUS NAME - AMEN

Devotion Day 5. Roles for Husband and Wife

The purpose of a role in any environment (work, church, school, or family) is to offer that person a clear path to success. In today's society, views of marital education have become more confused about the roles and purpose and mission than ever before. With the attack of the feminists and the redefinition of masculinity and sexuality, people are leaning more on their emotions than immovable truths to define their roles. You cannot escape the role of marriage as husband and wife. I grew up in a tradition home where Mum was seen in the kitchen and raised the family whist Dad was seen being the provider and handyman around the home. In marriage, it is helpful for each spouse to have a role that is recognised and valued with certain responsibilities to which he or she is held accountable. Deciding these roles should be a process whereby both the husband and wife mutually agree on assigning these responsibilities. In this way, each spouse makes a commitment to take care of something and is accountable to the other spouse for following through. While having both spouses involved in various responsibilities is beneficial, one still needs to take ownership. Responsibility involves action, follow through, and accountability. Defining roles and responsibilities is beneficial because it reduces the possibility for misunderstandings 'I thought you were going take care of that': blame *'I did my part, but you didn't'*: and criticism *'Why did you do it that way'?:* A clear assignment and definition of responsibilities reduces the opportunity for conflict and allows you to form healthy boundaries in your marriage. Boundaries help determine who is responsible for what. If you understand who owns (is responsible for) what, you then know who must take responsibility for it. Responsibilities in marriage are largely determined by a spouse's preferences, skills, interests, abilities, and time availability. Because of these variables, the definition of responsibilities will differ from couple to couple. While deciding on responsibilities is helpful, spouses should not be overly rigid about who does the tasks. If your spouse is overwhelmed and needs help taking care of his/her responsibilities, you should help bear one another's burdens (Galatians 6:2) while still attending to your own personal responsibilities (Galatians 6:5). When spouses feel support from each other during stressful times, trust and closeness are fostered. Spouses who work cooperatively, empower one another, help each other feel needed, and sometimes accomplish tasks more quickly (Ecclesiastes. 4:9). Problems can easily arise if the roles are not clearly defined, or too rigid. Responsibilities may need to shift from time to time. Effective, proactive communication can help you deal with these issues when they arise. If you approach marriage from a truly humble position of a servant, you will experience a divine union. Choose to live selflessly, your home will overflow with love, joy, peace, happiness and fulfilment. You'll give the world a picture of the love of God. I grew up with the phrase 'the bread-winner'. A term we rarely here as it has become little out of date yet, it is still applicable. However, I do not believe that a husband's provision for his wife is limited to finance. I believe that he is responsible for her total well-being: for example: physical, emotion, social and cultural, that he has to see that all her legitimate needs are met. In other words, if you want to know how successful a man is, look at his wife. She's the evidence. And when a wife is fully provided for in every area of her life, physical emotional, social and cultural, she will indeed be her husband's glory. The true measure of a mans heart is not what he earns, or the possessions he owns or the power he holds, or the professional successes achieved. The true measure of a mans heart is found in how much love he gives. How selflessly he shares whatever he can to help others. How consistent he is with lifting up those around him with a kind word or funny joke, a compliment as well as a humble ear to listen. The true measure of a man with these qualities is immeasurable. Turning now to the wife: What is her contribution to a successful marriage? God introduces marriage in Genesis 2, He describes what He intends the wife to be: *a helper*. There are two primary ways in which a wife can help her husband. The first is to **uphold,** the second is to **encourage.** Do you need to become more of an encourager to your husband? How often do you say, '*You can do it! I believe in you! You're the best!*'? How often do you notice his effort to make the yard look nice or to keep the cars running smoothly? When was the last time you said, '*You handled that situation so well*'? Or are you the chronic complainer? **Uphold** and **encourage.** In a nutshell - Marriage roles have evolved, encouraging couples embrace shared home responsibilities for deeper connection; let's value teamwork and recognise each other's efforts daily. Modern husbands thrive through emotional support and open communication, building a strong foundation for lasting partnership; this lead with love, understanding, and courage. Both couples make an equal investment for a happier, healthier relationship.

Devotional Questions Day 5
Your Roles

Who plays their roles best in your marriage? There is no 'I' in a team. Some couples like to share and take turns in their roles and responsibilities around the home. But, who plays each position best in your marriage? Some assignments and tasks may adapt over time, but overall who's better positioned right now to complete each task? Below are a few examples of a roster around the home.

Create your own roster for your home. Write down the different positions that need to be filled and assign the best player (spouse) to each role. Some tasks may be handed off to one spouse, whilst the other gets hardly any tasks at all. Try to range them from daily, weekly and monthly. Remember this is a fun task to create an opportunity to form a closer 'team' roles within your marriage.

Here are some examples: Paying the bills, car and maintenance, house hold budget, grocery shopping, laundry, gardening, dusting, cooking, mowing the lawn, cleaning and washing up after meals, driving kids to school and school pick up, planning a holiday, supervising homework, looks after the pets, cleans up after the pets, and general housework.

Husband list your roles here:

_____
_____
_____
_____
_____
_____

Wife list your roles here:

_____
_____
_____
_____
_____
_____

What were your first initial thoughts when entering into marriage? Did you enter into your marriage with any preconceived ideas about which tasks either of you should have or be responsible for? Do you see any areas in your relationship where adjustments are required?

_____
_____
_____
_____

Read 1 Peter 3:7 - Men, why is it important for you as a husband to view your wife as an equal spouse in your relationship. What will happen if your don't? Women, why is it important for you as a wife to not withhold honour from your husband? What will happen if you don't?

Jesus gave us the greatest example when He took the lowest portion of service and washed the decibels feet (John 13:1-7 NIV). Whilst the act of foot washing is absent in todays culture, the continual need to serve one another remains. Discuss some practical ways you can imitate Jesus and symbolically 'wash your spouses feet' (Serve).

A marriage between a husband and wife is meant to reflect the image of Jesus' relationship with us. His Bride. How do the husband's and wive's role's reveal the love of Jesus towards His church and towards unbelievers?

_____
_____
_____

What are your thoughts and feelings if the roles were refused. The wife goes to work and the dad stays at home?

_____
_____
_____

Pause and Pray

'LORD BLESS OUR MARRIAGE. SATISFY OUR DESIRE FOR HAPPINESS THROUGH THE AFFECTION AND ENCOURAGEMENT WE SHARE. TEACH US TO CARE AND SERVE EACH OTHER WELL. MAY WE BE CONTENT AS WE LIVE IN YOUR LOVE, AND THE JOY OF OUR MARRIAGE, EVERY DAY.
IN JESUS NAME - AMEN'

CHAPTER SEVEN
IN2MACY

'I have come into my garden, my sister, my bride; I have gathered my myrrh with my spice. I have eaten my honeycomb and my honey; I have drunk my wine and my milk. Friends eat, friends, and drink; drink your fill of love'.

- Song of Solomon 5:1 NIV

DEVOTION DAY 1

Sex! It's everywhere. It's on our televisions and in magazines. It's on the movie screens as well as our mobile devices, and computers. It's in the songs we sing and dance along to and in the latest celebrity scandals. Sex is used to sell everything from motor vehicles, food, clothes to deodorants. Ever since 'the sex revolution' of the '60s, each new generation has tried to outdo the one before it. Sex is indeed everywhere and unfortunately; it has become a cheap element and something that many struggle to truly understand the value of. Yet look where it's got us, nowhere. The love children of the sexual revolution have broken lives with broken hearts. Then came the arrival of HIV/AIDS. Most commonly transmitted through casual unprotected sex, each one craving what they called 'intimacy'. Scripture is not shy in describing God's plan for making love. In fact just spend a few moments reading the book of Song of Solomon with your spouse and see what happens. Today, modern couples get excited; even blush when the content of this love is taken in and understood. This book gives us a far deeper understanding and greater picture of an intimate relationship between a man and a woman. For example; the joys, the struggles as well as the complications, it's almost as if the life that this couple is exploring has a life of its own. The woman says several times in Song of Solomon 8:4, *'Do not stir up nor or awaken love until it pleases'*. It's almost as if she saying this love is so good, it's so beautiful, I don't want to mess this up. Unlike many of us, God is not ashamed of sex. He delights in its beauty and celebrates its whole purpose. God wants to be intimately involved in our INTIMACY, as you have learnt though reading chapter seven. God designed sex to be a power symbol and celebration of covenant love. It is a physical and emotional expression of the deepest commitment two people can make to each other. But sex is more than that. It represents the ultimate covenant love – God's love for His people.

I have heard stories where, husbands use Bible verses to guilt their wives into sex, saying that their wife isn't following what the Bible says if they don't submit to them sexually. I've also heard stories of wives using sex (or the lack of) to punish or reward their husbands for being their definition of a good husband. Some wives withhold sex as a form of control. When sex becomes selfish, controlling or manipulative, the results are disastrous, turning sex into something trivial and meaningless. But this isn't God's design. Sex is incredibly intimate and beautifully designed by God to connect spouses at the most intimate level. Anything in the bedroom needs to be between ONLY a husband and wife

> *'Drink water from your own cistern, running water from your own well. Should your springs overflow in the streets, your streams of water in the public squares? Let them be yours alone, never to be shared with strangers. May your fountain be blessed, and may you rejoice in the wife of your youth. A loving doe, a graceful deer, may her breasts satisfy you always, may you ever be intoxicated with her love'.*
>
> – Proverbs 5:15-19

This means that it's just a husband and his wife. No other people. No matter what. No exceptions. This isn't meant to hinder you or stop you from having fun in the bedroom. If anything, it's quite the opposite. God wants to protect the emotional health of your marriage and the covenant promise. He cares about us so much that He sets boundaries to protect the oneness of our marriages. With these boundaries in place, there is freedom to explore, have fun, and grow in intimacy with your spouse, with emotional and physical safety. God says that freedom should characterise the Christian life. So within a marriage, most things you do sexually are perfectly fine. Many Christians worry that new positions or new ways to touch or kiss may cross a line, but the marriage bed is undefiled. Fun is good! Let's make sure that in exercising that freedom, you don't inadvertently mimic our culture's distorted view of sex. Not everything you do is beneficial, especially if it makes sex only about the physical and not about a spiritual connection.

Ask yourselves: Are you living out your freedom in the bedroom? Are you living out that freedom in a way that's beneficial? Your intimacy just needs love, commitment, and laughter.

Day 1 Devotion questions
IN2MACY

God created sex before the fall in the Garden of Eden. Within marriage this was pleasing to God. There is no stronger bond of love and intimacy between a man and a woman.

What is your attitude towards sex in your marriage? Do you view it with a pure and positive design from God which He intended? Briefly describe your answer Why? Or Why not?

_____
_____
_____
_____
_____

Many of us have been told mixed views about sex, regardless of what you were taught in the past about sex, God wants you to know that He fully approves of and blesses your sexual union and intimate moments with your spouse. Be honest, how do you see sex fitting into the portrait of your marriage? Has it been something you have tolerated or something you have celebrated?

_____
_____
_____
_____

The most important aspect of sexual intimacy is honour. Is any of your current behaviour dishonouring your marriage bed?

_____
_____
_____
_____

Pause and Pray

'LORD BLESS OUR MARRIAGE. THANK YOU FOR THE BEAUTIFUL GIFT OF SEX. THANK YOU THAT YOU HAVE GIVEN US SEX AS A WAY TO GROW CLOSER TOGETHER, BUILD TRUST, RELIEVE STRESS, STRENGTHEN OUR BOND, AND CREATE CHILDREN. LORD, WE PRAY FOR HUSBANDS AND WIVES TO INTENTIONALLY WORK ON THEIR SEXUAL INTIMACY IN THEIR MARRIAGE. IN JESUS NAME - AMEN

DEVOTION DAY 2. FIVE STAGES OF INTIMACY

'Marriage should be honoured by all, and the marriage bed kept pure, for God will judge the adulterer and all the sexually immoral'.

- Hebrews 13:4 NIV

At times, we serve our spouse by having sex even when we don't feel sexy, or in the mood! Throw in a life threatening illness or physical disability and your vows *'for better for worse, in sickness in health'* takes on a whole new role. There are other ways we can show intimacy without having sex. This is pleasing to God. When we are intimate with one another, you are simply celebrating love with all five areas of intimacy.

Physical intimacy (non-sexual), is a way to express your affection and connection with your spouse. It can include things like holding hands, hugging, cuddling, or even a massage. For many of us physical intimacy or 'touch' is an important part within your marriage. It can help to build trust, foster communication, and deepen the bond between the both of you. It is important to remember that physical touch does not necessarily have to lead to having a sexual encounter. Many non-sexual forms of physical intimacy can be just as satisfying and meaningful. Think about your vows *'for better or for worse'* *'in sickness and in health'*. What if your wife or husband experiences an illness or has a physical disability. The only way of showing your deep affection towards each other is now through physical touch. Your bodies change and age over time, so does your style of intimacy, however the strength of your love between each other shouldn't diminish. Don't be afraid to express your affection in whatever way feels comfortable for you.

Emotional intimacy is a crucial part of a healthy marriage. It's what allows you to feel close to your spouse and to share your innermost thoughts and feelings. Unfortunately, many couples find it difficult to maintain emotional intimacy and one of the biggest predictors of divorce is a lack of emotional intimacy. Growing and developing an emotional intimate connection with your spouse will set you up for the long run! One way to do this is to make time for meaningful conversations regularly. This can be done by setting aside time each week to talk about your day, your thoughts, and your feelings.

Intellectual intimacy - is a special kind of relationship that allows partners to share their innermost thoughts and feelings with each other. This type of intimacy requires honesty, vulnerability, and a willingness to truly be seen by your partner. It is not about showboating or trying to impress each other with your intelligence; instead, it is about sharing your ideas and thoughts in a safe and trusting environment. If you are interested in deepening your relationship with your partner, make an effort to create opportunities for intellectual intimacy. Ask questions about their day, their work, and their thoughts on current events. The more you learn about each other, the closer you will become. One area where many couples struggle is the area of spiritual intimacy.

- For couples in the pre-married stage of life, this is the most important topic they need to discuss but often becomes the last area they talk about.

- For married couples, spiritual intimacy should be the backbone of their relationship but instead becomes something most couples don't even know how to discuss.

- And for couples who are struggling, this is the one thing they need to focus on and the one thing that can bring them back together. When we use the word intimacy, we often think of physical intimacy, (sex) .

While this is certainly an aspect of marital intimacy, it's not the only area.

Spiritual intimacy is that sense of soul-deep connection that allows you to be fully yourself with another person, and to feel loved and accepted for who you are. It's the kind of closeness that can only come from sharing your innermost thoughts and feelings, and from knowing that you are loved and supported, no matter what. Spiritual intimacy doesn't happen overnight. It takes time, effort, and a willingness to be vulnerable with each other. But the payoff is more than worth it. When you have spiritual intimacy in your relationship, you have a foundation of trust and mutual respect that can weather any storm. You know that you can always count on each other, no matter what happens. And that's the most priceless gift of all.

Sexual intimacy is the part of the relationship where couples connect on a physical and emotional level. It is an important way to show your partner that you love and care for them. It is also a great way to relieve stress and maintain a healthy physical relationship. When it comes to intimacy remember it is a fundamental needs for both a man and a woman, and it comes in many different forms, these 5 Levels of intimacy are all permissible in your marriage.

Day 2 Devotion questions
Five stages of intimacy

The language of intimacy can reveal many areas of physical activity without leading to sex. For example: words of affirmation, acts of service, quality time, receiving gifts, holding hands, kissing, cuddling, hugging, and playful touch. Our love language can fill our emotional, spiritual, physical, intellectual and sexual needs. Being aware of our physical limitations can often hinder the fulfilment of experiencing a full sexual encounter. As we age, we develop a mature approach to our intimacy desires. We still have to find time to nurture and serve each other. (Remember a woman's body goes through many changes throughout her life - she is known as the 'life bearer'). Having an open, honest dialogue with your partner is key to building intimacy and keeping your intimacy life exciting. This isn't about prying or putting your partner on the spot. It's about creating a safe space to communicate what you need physically and emotionally.

Husband, are you giving more time and attention to your work or children than you give to your wife?

What can you do to better serve her physical needs? Humble yourself and openly communicate with your wife about what she likes, get her input, then pray about this together.

_____
_____
_____

How important is sex in a relationship to you? This reveals how aligned you both are on sexual needs. Neither view is right or wrong if discussed respectfully.

_____
_____
_____

Do you have any specific sexual fears or anxieties that you'd like to address? Addressing sexual fears and anxieties openly can create a safe space for vulnerability and growth in the relationship.

_____
_____
_____

The bedroom should remain your private sanctuary. A place where you both become one flesh. The most common bedroom passion distractions surround the following examples:

Personal Hygiene and Appearance: Poor hygiene, such as body odour, bad breath, or dirty nails, can be a major turn-off. Unkempt appearance, including worn-out underwear, can also dampen the mood.

External Factors: Excessive checking of social media during intimacy can disrupt the moment.
Living with family or other distractions in the bedroom environment can hinder intimacy. Work stress, lack of sleep, or financial concerns can spill over into the bedroom.

Relationship Dynamics: Lack of communication about sexual needs and preferences can lead to frustration and dissatisfaction. Negative communication patterns, like excessive swearing or criticism, can damage intimacy. Feeling unappreciated or unloved can significantly impact sexual desire. Routine and predictability in the bedroom can lead to boredom.

Individual Factors: Loss of physical fitness or rapid weight changes can affect self-esteem and desire. Excessive alcohol consumption or smoking can impact both physical and emotional intimacy.

Using the list of examples, describe with each other what is working for you, and what is not. How could you do things better in the bedroom?

_____
_____
_____
_____
_____
_____
_____
_____
_____
_____
_____
_____
_____
_____

What are your thoughts and understanding on having sex before and after marriage?

_____
_____
_____
_____

How important is physical attraction to you in a sexual relationship? Understanding your partner's perspective on physical attraction can help you navigate the evolving dynamics of a relationship.

_____
_____
_____
_____

Are there any cultural or religious beliefs that influence your sexual desires or boundaries?

_____
_____
_____
_____

How do you feel about integrating non-sexual physical intimacy, like cuddling or hand-holding, into our daily routine? Physical touch outside of sexual contexts can help build emotional connection and increase desire. Discussing this can ensure you're meeting your partner's needs.

_____
_____
_____

How does stress affect your sexual desire, and how can your spouse help alleviate it? Stress can have a significant impact on libido. Understanding how it affects your partner and learning ways to reduce it can improve your sex life. Write your thoughts below.

_____
_____
_____

How has childbirth or health changes impacted your sexual comfort and confidence? Be compassionate around changing bodies. Discuss and pray together.

_____
_____
_____

Devotion Day 3. Marriage Vs. Disability

The love that carries a couple to the altar is not the same love that sustains them through the waves of marriage. Juggling family, careers, and finances. One of the things my husband and I did not talk about before marriage was the topic of future sex life and what each expected it to look like. We didn't take in, or consider, what our intimacy would look like should one of us fall ill. The unexpected challenges of living with a disability, can leave you exhausted and overwhelmed. Yet despite any hardships, you are called to live in humility, considering others' needs before your own. You are to *'have the attitude of Christ'*. Yet we live in a world that reinforces a *me-first* mindset. If I don't look after myself first, how can I look after my spouse. You've probably heard the saying that we must first put on our own oxygen mask so we can then help others. This is true, but we must be wary that self-care doesn't become self-centredness. Most marriages have an ebb and flow, with seasons of give and take. However, when one spouse has a disability, the other is often required to serve as the primary caregiver. This can lead to feelings of resentment, anger, or even depression. Self-centredness on the part of either spouse is detrimental to a healthy marriage and is not the example Christ modelled. You need to find what works well for you both. You may find after years of giving birth, your body isn't responding to sexual feelings like it used to. Any form of major surgery can impact how you express your intimacy with each other. Are sexual toys allowed? I'd encourage you to explore what works best for you. As long as its done without shame or pain and does not lead to sexual immorality.

In Philippians 2:3-8, Paul emphasises the sacrificial nature of Christ's love for us and challenges us to do likewise. In Ephesians 5, Paul reiterates this call to Christ-likeness, and then proceeds to apply the concept to marriage. He teaches mutual submission, where each spouse is willing to go the *'extra mile'* for the other. By contrast, the world promotes marriage as a partnership, an 'equitable' relationship with a 50/50 split of benefits, burdens, and responsibilities. However life, and marriage doesn't always go how we planned.

How can we combat the human tendency to 'look out for number one'? Through prayer. God not only understands your unique needs but also tells you to come boldly to Him. He asks you to lay any resentment, anger, anxiety, or fear at His feet, so that He can pour His love and mercy into your life. Couples coping with pain, disease, hardship, or mental illness need to constantly pray together, asking for the same attitude that Christ had when He humbled himself to obey God's plan. He gives us access to come before the throne of grace and promises to show us the way forward.

Sex and disability: Most people have sexual thoughts, attitudes, feelings and desires. Having a physical, terminal illness or intellectual disability doesn't change that but disabilities can impact on sex. What to do if sex isn't working for you? Couples who live with a disability have the right to have a sexual relationship. Yet young people living with a disability often have numerous barriers to attaining good sexual health and wellbeing. It is commonly assumed that they don't or can't have sex.

What is a disability? A disability can be any number of physical or mental chronic illnesses, impairments or differences that substantially and frequently limits one or more major life activities For example: Not being able to communicate your needs and desires, doing basic self-care, processing information cognitively, keeping a job or traveling, eating or sleeping. A given disability may be about or impact mobility, cognitive function, sight, speech/language, hearing or more than one of those things. Just like it's hard to create one, all encompassing definition for sex that fits everyone, the same is true for a disability, so not everyone disabled shares the same definition. Yet, we all desire the one love that comes from God. Disabilities shouldn't keep you from love and marriage and, if at all possible, sexual intimacy.

You have learnt that a strong marriage is essential. But somewhere along the way, expectations collided with real life and your hopes and dreams gave way to hindrances and obstacles that began to make marriage hard. Without it, caring for someone with special needs is that much more difficult and challenging. Combine high frustration levels with tumultuous emotions, medical concerns, behaviour problems, housing considerations and family and other relationship issues, and it appears to be a job with no end. Where is God in all of this?

Perfection is not required of any of us. We all have challenges. Embrace the body you have and the wonderful things you can do with it. You may need some adaptation to get it done, but you are *'fearfully and wonderfully made'* (Psalm 139:14).

Day 3 Devotion Questions
Marriage Vs. Disability

God loves you both. He wants your marriage to succeed. The question is, what expectations do you now have for your marriage? What God inspired possibilities are you praying and believing for?

_____
_____
_____
_____
_____
_____
_____
_____

Take time together and meditate on the following passages:...

...'For when you did awesome things that we did not expect, you came down, and the mountains trembled before you. Since ancient times no one has heard,

no ear has perceived, no eye has seen any God besides you, who acts on behalf of those who wait for him'.
 - Isaiah 64:3-4 NIV

...'The unfolding of your words gives light, it gives understanding to the simple. I open my mouth and pant, longing for your commands. Turn to me and have mercy on me, as you always do to those who love your name'.
 - Psalm 119:130-132 NIV

Describe your 'In sickness and in health' Describe your own health condition? Are there sexual obstacles that need addressing?

_____
_____
_____
_____
_____
_____
_____
_____
_____

Devotion Day 4. Pornography Vs. Intimacy

Satan is after Sex! As you have learned over the past few chapters. God designed sex to be a power symbol and celebration of covenant love. It is a physical and emotional expression of the deepest commitment two people can make to each other. But sex is more than that. It represents the ultimate covenant love – God's love for His people.

Because sex is a portrait of God's sacred love, Satan will do anything he can to destroy the beauty of it. He has tried to twist, tarnish, and distort the beautiful and holy picture of sexuality in every way possible. Sexual immorality, such as sexual addiction, porn, prostitution, sexual abuse, sexual pain, gender confusion, these are all examples of how Satan keeps Christians from ever celebrating sexuality within the context of God's Holy Design. Sex has been dragged through the mud so thoroughly that most people can't even comprehend that it is intended to be something holy. It is key for you to recognise Satan's assaults on your sexuality and your marriage. You may be carrying around guilt and sexual shame, but never have identified the source. Satan's agenda is to destroy, discourage, and defeat the Christian marriage bed. Your spouse, your past, even pornography are not the primary culprit. Satan has used these tools toward his agenda of defiling the good gift of sex.

The good news is found in I John 4:4 - *'Greater is He that is in you than He that is in the world'*.

You don't have to be a statistic – another marriage wrecked by porn, another woman permanently scarred by abuse, or another couple who fights endlessly about sex.

Satan's schemes cannot stand against the word and the power of God. So often, God's truth is ignored related to sexuality. When you study what God has to say about forgiveness, redemption and His design for sex, the enemy will be defeated! However, on the other hand, the reality of God has darkened people's views in the life-flow of modern culture, an exchange of truth for an illusion of spiritual pleasure has occurred. The illusion is that humans have a right to self-pleasure, and especially playing with sex. After all, we are entitled to pursue happiness right? Whilst this exchange is being played out, God and the Bible are portrayed as opponents to the quest for pleasure, and this is where this whole 'illusion' gets messy.

We have been told that the pursuit of pleasure with our bodies is the road to happiness.

However, ignoring God's design and direction for sexual activity comes at a high price. Sexual activity is not a safe pursuit outside of marriage. Sexual sin comes wrapped and gifted in the illusion of self-pleasure. Sexual sin such as pornography looks desirable and fun, but just as the Proverbs warn, the aftermath is devastating. Sadly the existence of porn is killing and destroying the true look of intimacy. There's absolutely nothing wrong for couples wanting to explore their sexuality within the context of their marriage. However, the moment 'pornography' gets involved it ends up destroying the love that is sadly becoming an uncomfortable pleasure where couples relationships are being robbed and tainted with the wrong vision. Porn is simply false love! When a couple bring porn into their union, they defile their marriage bed by including others into their intimacy. This was never Gods plan.

The sexual experience should be a reminder of the covenant that joins two lives. You marital covenant has no room for a third party. The temptation to explore porn usually starts around adolescence. Thus, believing the idea that porn, like the drugs heroin, ice, cocaïne, alcohol and tobacco, not only gives you temporary pleasure, but it robs you of long-term health, satisfaction, and joy. Porn is just as addictive as heroin and cocaine. It spikes dopamine levels with the same ferocity as many narcotics. While it promises sexual virility and freedom, it delivers sexual chains and frustration. Doctors are prescribing Viagra to guys in their 20's with a history of porn use because they've trained their brain to be satisfied by pixels more, than their spouse.

These facts alone won't change a person's heart. For the vast majority of people, don't suffer from temporary amnesia when they look at pornography. You enter into every session of this temptation with full knowledge knowing this will damage your relationship not only with your loving God, but with the person you are dating, engaged too or married. The book of 1 Corinthians 6:18 say'; *'Flee from sexual immorality. All other sins a person commits are outside the body, but whoever sins sexually, sins against their own body'.* We look at the naked pictures because we want to. We believe those fleeting pixels will satisfy us, cure our loneliness, or be a soothing balm for our insecurities far more than God can. We can't just sit back and pretend to think there's an easy answer to fight the battle against pornography. At least with smoking or drugs society has made a decision to create legal, economic, and social barriers to getting hooked. Thanks to the internet, we've removed all obstacles to porn. This may be the first vice in history that is instantly accessible, affordable, and culturally acceptable for everyone as long as you can access the internet. Jesus said in John 8:32, *'The truth will set you free'.* Then later Jesus said, *'Truly, truly I say to you, everyone who commits sin is a slave to sin...if the Son sets you free, you will be free indeed'.* Pornography is like any sin. It slowly enslaves us when we believe our secret glances will satisfy us more than Jesus. Almost everything we think we know about addiction is wrong. Let's take a deeper look at this devotion; for example: You buy a mouse, you put the mouse in a cage and give it two water bottles. One bottle is pure water and the other is laced with a drug. If you do this the mouse will almost, always prefer the water laced with the drug and it will slowly kill itself quickly. If you look at this scenario with the mouse and wonder why the mouse is slowly dying, you'll soon discover that your mouse is bored, its in an empty cage with no toys to stimulate its physical or mental health. Its got nothing except to use these drugs. If you add toys, loads of cheese, coloured balls, mouse wheels and other fun activities for the mouse, add 2-3 other mice for friends. What happens is, your mouse no longer likes the drug water. You go from 100% overdose when your isolated to 0% when you have happier and connected lives. What if, this addiction resembles your pornography addition? What if, you addiction to porn is about your cage? Your environment. Maybe we shouldn't call it an *addiction,* maybe we should call it *bonding.* Human beings have a natural need to bond. When we are happy and healthy we will bond and connect with each other. However if you can't to this, because you have experienced trauma or have been feed lies about sex, lust, and have been shown the wrong images by false friends, almost always you will beat yourself down with isolation with a cheap pornographic image that will give you some sort of short false relief.

No matter how far into your marriage, no matter what struggles you face along your journey, at some point the enemy will tempt you where your eyes and ears will feel the pull in the opposite direction, away from Gods path because that's our nature. The opposite of pornography addiction is connection. Jesus invites you to connect with Him.

You know the scenario: The room is empty. You're alone. You look over at your folded laptop sitting idle on the desk, and the urge for sexual release that has been intensifying all day collides with the seductive thought of indulging in porn yet again. You think to yourself, *'I know it's sin, I know I'll feel horrible afterwards, I know the satisfaction won't last'*. And yet, so often the scenario ends with turning on the computer, typing in a website's URL, and taking part in the dark porn experience again. Victory over porn is not a call to mere self-denial, but a call to exuberant indulgence in the person and work of Jesus Christ. Next time the dreary clouds of lust come over your room, set your mind on what Jesus is doing to you, and for you, in that very moment. Set your mind upon the things of Christ (Romans 8:5-6; Colossians 3:2), and may your joy in Jesus become too fulfilling, too gratifying, too satisfying to forfeit over to the sad counterfeit pleasure of pornography.

When we sin against God, we are actively biting the hand that is presently feeding us. When we rebel against God, we are striking the Physician that is offering, in that very moment, the life-sustaining medicine. 1 John 1:9 reads; *'If we confess our sins, he is faithful and just to forgive us our sins and to cleanse us from all unrighteousness'*. Let's be honest, overcoming addiction isn't a walk in the park. If you've reached out for help in the past, you may have been given advice such as, 'Just stop watching porn'. It's not always helpful. I pray these steps listed below gives you a place to start!

1. **Pursue intimacy with God.**
2. **Discover your trigger(s).**
3. **Discover your root issue(s).**
4. **Understand porn's impact on your brain.**
5. **Don't go through this alone.**

There are plenty of ways you can justify it: *'At least I'm not committing adultery'*. Or: *'There's worse stuff I could be viewing'*. But you're called to be a vessel of purity and righteousness unto God. His Word in Ephesians 5:3 is clear: *'But among you there must not be even a hint of sexual immorality, or of any kind of impurity, or of greed, because these are improper for God's holy people'*. A healthy marital life is not simply an immediate transformational encounter, but a lifelong journey of surrender and becoming more like Christ. While this is true for every area of your life, let's apply it specifically to your struggle with pornography. What does it practically look like for you to surrender your addiction to the Jesus?

Where can you find support for overcoming an addiction?
Joining a support group, Bible study, or community group will give you mental health support as you continue on this journey. https://www.beyondblue.org.au 24/7 Support or call
1300 22 4636

Day 4 Devotion questions
Pornography Vs. intimacy

The purity of your marriage is ultimately about the purity God desires in His Bride. Sexual desires aren't bad, they are Gods creation and He celebrates them! However when the wrong desires, actions or influences cripple your union, they war against intimacy and prevent what God has called good. The key to cultivating the correct desires is to share your human nature and feed your spirit. What you and your spouse take in with your eyes and ears you ultimatly take into your mind and heart. Your eyes and ears are the gateway to your spirit and soul. Everything you see and hear feeds you. Either in human nature or in spirit.

STOP! and **THINK.** In what ways are you feeding your human spirit? What are you watching? What are you listening to? Is your music, TV shows or movies adding fuel to your spirit? Are you feeding off books, magazines, social media, websites that area polluting your mind and falsifying your idea of what true love and intimacy is? Who influences you? Who holds you accountable for your addiction? Are any of them encouraging the wrong attitudes or actions?

_____
_____
_____
_____
_____

How are you feeding your spirit the truth of Gods Word about sex, intimacy and Holiness? Pray and ask the Holy Spirit to show you practical ways to feed your spirit and cultivate the right desires.

_____
_____
_____
_____
_____
_____
_____
_____

Devotion Day 5. Intimacy with God

Your marriage and your intimate relationship with God is the substance of christianity. It is the foundation of all spirituality. It is the purpose for Jesus' sacrifice, the culmination of the scriptures, the bedrock of your life. Everything you do, think, experience and believe is rooted in the quietly of the relationship. Knowing what kind of relationship God is looking for, understanding what the terms of this relationship are, and knowing what kind of person you are entering a marriage with are essential parts of getting the most out of that relationship. The Bible uses the metaphor of marriage on several occasions to draw a picture of the relationship between God and mankind. I love this because it beautifully captures the intimacy, mystery and progression of a relationship with God. We are always discovering more of who He is, more of how He loves us, and more on how we can love Him. Is intimacy with God possible? Knowing Jesus is supposed to cure our loneliness, give us purpose in life and help calm our fears. While an intimate relationship with God is presented as a cure all for both now and eternity, few marriages actually know what intimacy with God practically means. As we face the fears of losing loved ones, possessions or jobs, do we really know God well enough for Him to be all that we have? Is it even possible to have that deep and meaningful of a relationship with the living God? God told the Israelites in Jeremiah 29:13 NIV: *'You will seek Me and find Me when you search for Me with all your heart'.* I believe that same promise is for your marriage. God can use your current circumstances to awaken in us a desire for more of Him. When we seek more of Him, we will have more of Him. Intimacy with God will become a regular priority when you believe it is absolutely critical for both of you to function. When I fully surrender to the work of God in me, *good* works through me in every aspect of my life. My marriage is blessed, my family is blessed, my ministry life is blessed. Everything is covered by the blood of Jesus. I need His direction. I need His perspective. I need His love, I am lost without Him. What, in your life is impossible to do without being connected to God?

I sing. I like to sing out loud in the car. And I do mean loud. Sometimes I literally weep for the joy of being on an adventure with God. With each mile and each song, the tensions from the week wash away. This is just one area where I like to spend time with God. In that moment, its like I'm running away for a day with the One who loves me most, and life is very, very good. The drive becomes a spiritual journey. I love different genre's of music, every word is heard, every harmony enjoyed. The drive is part of the time spent with the Lord. It's musical prayer. It's heart readjustment. It's surrender and a reminder and victory depending on the song. The worship sets the tone for the day, and it's so nice to sing and focus on God.

When the weather allows, I walk beside the ocean, admiring waves crashing on the beach, and seagulls hovering overhead. I sit. I admire. I listen. God stills my soul, and we are together. Its just He and I, in the midst of His creation. It's a day with a simple agenda: be with God, love, and be loved. The renewal and the resetting of priorities occurs each time I 'stop' and recalibrate my heart.

There are times my husband and I share in this precious time together. Getting away from all the distractions fighting for your attention and just listening is the most challenging and rewarding thing you will ever do to discover your purpose. It is truly the greatest private habit a couple can do. Make time to be alone, and be quiet to listen.

God wants to give you the healing, the wisdom, the direction you so desperately desire. He wants to reveal His next steps for your life. Do you need a devotional time makeover? Has your quiet time with God gotten lost in the daily busyness of life? Without knowing quite how it happens, your day can slip away into the night taking your God-time with it. Been there, done that. Actually, we've all let the cares of this world and the crazy busyness of life push aside our time with God. Unfortunately, each time we let it happen, it seems to get easier and easier to push aside again the next time. The good news is that God will gently call you back to him. At that point, you have a decision to make; you can choose to ignore Him or you can choose to grab your Bible and join Him once again for daily fellowship.

Maybe you are going through this now and God is calling to you through this devotion. But maybe you have never committed to having quiet, devotional time with God. Maybe you are a new Christian and aren't even sure what 'devotional time' even means. Or maybe the quiet time you have planned isn't working out as you thought and you need to rethink your plan. He wants to whisper insights and creative concepts. But, as we see in scripture, you must get quiet and alone to listen. Take time today and intentionally listen to God.

Let's make space for Him!

'Be still and know that I am God'

- Psalm 46:10

Day 5 Devotion Questions
Intimacy with God

Without question, freedom from sin is found in intimate fellowship with Jesus. How would you describe your relationship with Him?

_____
_____
_____
_____
_____
_____
_____
_____

How often do you give God your undivided time and attention?

_____
_____
_____
_____
_____
_____
_____
_____

What motivates you to seek His presence?

_____
_____
_____
_____
_____
_____

What directs most of your prayers, your desire for other things or your desire to know God?

_____
_____
_____
_____
_____
_____

Be still and listen to the Holy Spirit together. Write down and ask God for the grace to do what He says.

_____
_____
_____
_____
_____

If you could hear what you were wanting to hear from God right now, what would He say?

_____
_____
_____

The things that keep me from putting God first:

_____
_____
_____

Along those lines, how do you naturally enjoy God? Is it on a walk, or through art, or advocating for the disadvantaged, or sharing a soul-filling meal with true friends? How can you attach your natural motivations to our fulfilment in God?

_____
_____
_____
_____
_____
_____
_____

In order to cultivate an intimate relationship with God, In what areas of your life do you most struggle to believe in God's character? Put another way: In what ways do you most struggle with fear right now? Take time to explore, pray through, and perhaps record the underlying reasons and concerns threaded through those fears...and truths from God's Word about those specific fears.

_____
_____
_____
_____
_____
_____
_____
_____
_____
_____
_____
_____
_____
_____

One of the best ways to connect and experience a deeper intimate relationship with God is by experiencing new levels of freedom. Getting away as a married couple on a retreat or a small vacation allows focus time, prayer and communion with Him. A few days alone with God - disconnected from the distractions that demand your attention in the day-to-day, can forever transform your life and marriage. Find time to get away with God, put it on your calendar and make it a priority. Bring no agenda, no distractions - just You, your Bible, a journal and pen. Be ready to receive abundantly from the goodness and greatness of His heart!

Discover more intimate moments through reading:

1 Chronicles 16:27.

Psalm 16:11, 27:4-6, 31:19-20, 91:1-16.

Isaiah 40:31.

John 15:4-8.

Hebrews 4:16.

Do you like alone time? Or do you avoid it?

_____
_____
_____

Spending time with God allows us to grow deeper with Him. As you meditate on a passage of scripture or 'word' Here are 4 questions to tune your heart as you grow your knowledge and understanding. Ask yourself:

1. What am I feeling?
2. What does the passage speak too me?
3. What is God's invitation to me?
4. How will you respond?

Pause and Pray

'LORD BLESS OUR MARRIAGE. THANK YOU, FOR CARING ABOUT MY MOST INTIMATE THOUGHTS AND THE DESIRES OF MY HEART. GROW MY PASSION FOR PRAYER AND SPENDING TIME WITH YOU. HELP ME TO CHERISH MY TIMES WITH YOU, NO MATTER WHAT IS GOING ON IN MY LIFE. HELP ME TO STAY WHERE YOU WANT ME TO BE.

IN JESUS NAME - AMEN

Chapter Eight

Start With The End in Mind

'To begin with the end in mind means to start with a clear understanding of your destination. It means to know where you're going so that you better understand where you are now and so that the steps you take are always in the right direction'.

- Stephen R. Covey

Devotion Day 1

Movies and romantic novels appear to focus on the beginning of the love story. Take a moment and think of your favourite movie. What is the story line? Is it filled with emotional tension expressed with a dance of romantic courtship? Are you glued to the edge of your seat as the story line takes turns and twists that keep the two lovers from encountering their first kiss? Of course there's always the competitor, arguments, or unexpected trauma, however the story unfolds we all know how it will ultimately end. Despite the challenges that tried to keep them apart, these bright-eyed love-birds find a way to conquer their love for each other and the movie closes with…'And they lived happily ever after', but how? A fairy tale beginning is the easy part. The hard work comes in crafting the story's middle and end. When it comes to committing ourselves to someone for life, our vision and plans for our future are often not what God has planned for us. Jeremiah 29:11 reads; *'For I know the plans I have for you, declares the Lord, plans to prosper you and not to harm you, plans to give you hope and a future'.* I began my relationship with the end in mind. What this did was make me focus on building our marriage from day one centerings God love and people of knowledge and influence around us that would embrace and encourage us through what ever life offered. Every decision my husband and I made as a couple had a clear outcome: Moving house, changing jobs, starting a family, even building our own home. From the start our marriage resembled a builders 'blueprint'. We had the plans, now we just needed to contract our marital life the way God designed it. In marriage, whenever you have a vision for your life together, there is an action and process that takes place. You are actually visualising it twice: first in your mind, when you imagine it, and then physically, when you live. In our example, we first needed to visualise what kind of marriage wanted. Our vision was to have built our relationship on Gods foundation, adding in effective communication, mutual respect, trust, forgiveness, honesty, love, romance, quality time, goals, and to become 'one' with each other.

God gives you the ability to be proactive and to visualise things before they happen as a way to prepare yourselves before taking action. How does God ask us to visualise? If God grants you a dream or a vision for your marital journey, or Jesus paints a parable for a way to lead your marriage, or the Bible tells a story that inspires a new venture, this is what God wants you to visualise. You wouldn't dream of building a home without any blueprints, after all without the blueprints your new home would be structurally unsound! Every beautiful home begins with a well thought out plan and design. It's only after the plan is drafted that the builders can contract the house, doing so with hard work and the correct tools and right materials. Blueprints are also an essential material for determining the cost of construction. Would you be comfortable building your first home without first knowing how much it will cost you? Jesus reveals this thought when teaching us how to build our lives: *'Suppose one of you wants to build a tower. Won't you first sit down and estimate the cost to see if you have enough money to complete it? For if you lay the foundation and is not able to finish it, everyone who sees it will ridicule you, saying', 'This person began to build and wasn't able to finish it'* (Luke 14:28-30 NIV). God gave Abraham a vision of the stars of the sky and told him he would have that many children, and that, produced faith in Abraham's heart (Genesis 15:5-6). So, here we have an example of godly imagery which produced faith in the man who is called 'the Father of Faith' (Romans 4:11). God gave to Abraham, a spoken promise (Genesis 12:1,2) and a divine picture (Genesis 15:1,5,6). As you hold your promise and vision for your marriage in your heart, meditate on it and ponder it, God produces a miracle in the fullness of time. Take the time required for visualisation. First, make sure it is God-inspired. Better to ask God now than to lose your way pursuing what could be a toxic relationship. It's much more productive to spend time in prayer, meditation and thanksgiving anticipating an action and visualising the desired outcome, then just plowing hastily on, possibly in the wrong direction. Always start with the end in mind.

The whole concept of 'beginning with the end in mind' is not something I came up with. Its a term often described by management, a statement to simply manage one's life. It is a great concept and fits excellent when starting a new relationship.

Beginning with the end in mind means identifying what you want, and to be true to yourself or what you both want to accomplish at the end or what lays ahead of you.

As a wife, I want to know at the end of each study lesson, that I have grown in Christ, such as in character and conduct. I want to know that I am demonstrating more love, joy, peace, patience, kindness, goodness, gentleness, faithfulness, and self-control. When you 'begin with the end in mind' in anything - especially your relationship, the bottom line is to develop a plan to help you become the person God wants you to be. It helps you identify what you want to be true of your life and then work a plan to ensure you develop in each area. When stating over, beginning with the end in mind, or having a vision, is important.

I invite you to participate in a thought experiment with me. Imagine that you find yourself in a rowboat in the middle of a calm ocean, with no sign of land in any direction. You look north, south, east, and west and see no evidence of life or land.

Question: How fast would you row that boat? Why? Now imagine that in one direction, in the distance, you see some land. How fast and how hard would you row then? What's the difference? Proverbs 29:18 reads *'where there is no vision, the people perish'.* Why do couples perish without a vision? Because without a vision, we either stop rowing the boat or row in directions that take us to unintended places with unintended consequences. Great marriages have a clear vision of the end of any endeavour. God says in His Word 'where there is no vision, the people perish' (Proverbs 29:18). The same can be said for marriages. If you do not have a vision, a plan and a goal for your marriage, your marriage will perish.

It is therefore important to have a vision for your marriage from the onset so that when you go through the troubled and challenging times, and believe me you will have those times, you can hold onto that vision of 'wholeness', believe that eventually you will attain that vision and then work towards receiving it. God's vision for marriage is for your marriage to be a blessed one.

Day 1 Devotion questions

Start with the end in mind

What good is a journey without a destination? Sure, you might get to see a few things and go for a ride, but ultimately, the destination is the purpose. Marriage is a journey and it has a destination.

What type of marriage are you constructing?
_____
_____
_____
_____
_____
_____

Begin with the end in mind. Define a clear end goal to work toward so you live purposefully and prioritise actions that make a difference. Describe your end goal.
_____
_____
_____
_____
_____
_____

Put first things first. Prioritise tasks based on importance instead of urgency. Carefully choose those tasks that align with your long-term goals. List some of your priorities together. What is important? What requires urgent attention in your relationship?

_____
_____
_____
_____

Starting over again and making things new, starts with ourselves. Invest in becoming a better version of yourself physically, emotionally, mentally, and spiritually. How are you applying these habits day-to-day?

_____
_____
_____
_____

Pause and Pray

'LORD BLESS OUR MARRIAGE. WE ASK THAT YOU WOULD PROVIDE US WITH DISCERNMENT IN THE CHOICES WE NEED TO MAKE. IF THERE'S A SPECIFIC PATH YOU WANT US TO TAKE. HELP US TO HAVE THE COURAGE TO TAKE THE STEP YOU'RE LEADING US TOWARD.

IN JESUS NAME - AMEN

Devotion Day 2. Having fun in your marriage

Are you having fun in your marriage? It sounds like a ridiculous question, doesn't it? After all, most of us got married because we liked being together and doing fun things. However, after a few years of marriage, many of us don't even think about fun. We are just trying to get through the day keeping up with a household of kids, finding money to pay bills, and figuring out how to be at two different places at once … Who has time for fun in marriage?

Yes, life has its share of disappointments, debts, unexpected challenges and trials. We all get drained of energy. Yet like a shaft of sunlight, fun and laughter can illuminate our world by reminding us life is not supposed to be so serious. A Christian marriage ought to be found guilty of having too much wholesome fun rather than too little. Marriages that stop enjoying each other can hold the potential of slowly slipping into routine and boredom. Playfulness refreshes our souls and lifts us out of the daily ruts. It drives away the drab, dull, and the mundane. It lightens our loads and knits our hearts together.

Have you ever laughed at yourself? Humour is essential to fun. When we don't take ourselves too seriously it allows our spouse to enjoy the moment, and get a little flirtatious. Please note: there is a fine line between laughing *at* and laughing *with* our spouse. So please be self-aware and conscious about how your humour is being received! Are you laughing *with* your spouse or *at* your spouse?

When was the last time you did something fun together? I frequently encourage couples to have more shared activities. I'm not referring to chores! My husband and I enjoy leisurely hikes and walks along the pristine beaches.

Doing sports together can be fun as well, one just has to be mindful about our spouse's skill and endurance levels, otherwise it's not a great experience! Sometimes simple joys can be found around us. One of the perks of working from home together is being able to enjoy a short break at what what ever cafe you choose. It's the laughter and warm, fuzzy feelings that make the day so much more enjoyable and memorable. After a challenging season early in our marriage we've learned a few ways to keep things fun. For us, it all comes down to getting out of the house, walks, coffee and God. This means doing something together. We share in healthy conversation,

...and we laugh at ourselves along the way. Do you have fun in marriage together? I hope the answer is an all-capital-letters YES! Having fun in marriage matters.

If you've been married for awhile, you might feel like you're past the 'having fun' part of it all. Not at all, friend!
The reality is, having fun in marriage does matter. It makes you a happier person, it reflects the goodness of God to a broken world, and it shows your kids what a happy marriage looks like. You become of influence. They are going to desire the happy marriage you model.
Marriage can start to revolve around managing the kids, paying the bills, handling chores... and while you can make those things more fun, that's not the first place to start!
Playing together increases bonding, communication, conflict resolution, and relationship satisfaction. Play can also promote spontaneity when life seems routine, serve as a reminder of positive relationship history, and promote intimacy. Having fun together can help couples feel positive emotions, which can increase relationship satisfaction, help couples to unite in order to overcome differences and give hope when working through difficult challenges. Some studies have even found that having fun together is the most important factor in the sense of

friendship, commitment, and the greatest influence on overall marital satisfaction. Consider what is blocking you from having fun and discuss what you are willing to do about this with your spouse. It may also be helpful to brainstorm a list of things you want to try or things you think are fun that you want to do again. At this point, don't worry about cost or time, the sky is the limit! Write it on your calendar and follow through with your play date. Be sure to schedule play dates often and take turns choosing the activities that you can both agree on. Strong, healthy, happy, and long lasting relationships do not just happen, they require effort.

Laughter is a gift from God. It can brighten any day and lift heavy hearts. Seniors often carry wisdom gained through life's challenges, but they also deserve moments of pure joy. Humour has a unique way of connecting us to each other and to God. It reminds us not to take ourselves too seriously.

Every relationship needs a little fun. Be intentional about having fun in your relationship. You will find greater happiness in your relationship and life in general.

Day 2 Devotion questions
Having fun in your marriage

Is your marriage fun? For a lot of people, this question is a no-brainer. 'Of course we're having fun'! they say. Yet for many, this question makes some couples realise it's been a long time since 'fun' has been a word to describe their marriage. Too often we get stuck in the grind of life and forget there's a season for everything – including laughter! The good news is you don't need to be a comedian to bring the fun back into your marriage.

Work through the list of fun topics to create open and healthy discussion between yourself and your spouse or even in an encouraging group setting. Place a mark next the ones that inspire you to have fun with your spouse. Remember there's always room for fun and laughter.

- Be spontaneous and flirty
- Do new things together

- Create something together
- Expect surprises

- Go dancing together
- Play games

- Art Gallery tours.
- Attend a festival or concert

- Cook dinner together
- Date each other

- Daydream together
- Enjoy a romantic getaway

- Go stargazing
- Massage your partner

- Recreate your first date
- Serve Together

- Try new hobbies together
- Be affectionate

'Rejoice in the Lord always; again I will say, rejoice'
— Philippians 4:4 ESV

Devotion day 3. The Bride of Christ

A bride-to-be can stand motionless in front of the mirror for what appears to be an eternity. For any girl who has dreamt of this day, she can work hard to prepare for this very moment. Her hair can reveal a work of art, her makeup looks immaculate, never before has she felt so beautiful. In the Jewish culture when a bride became engaged, that became the start of their marriage from that day on. There was no consummation of the marriage yet, but back then, you were known as 'betrothed'.

The Bride of Christ is seen in the Ten Commandments. In Jewish culture they wrote what is known as a *'cotubai'*. Todays traditional vows speak of putting each other first before anyone else. 'You will be the only one'. So when we look at the Ten Commandments, this is Gods *cotubai* to us. These are His vows. If we come together and vow our love for one another, the result of this obedience is a guarantee to have a beautiful and fruitful marriage. The Ten Commandments play an interesting role when you get married, God said; *'I am the*

Lord your God who brought you out of the land of Egypt the house of bondage'.

If we look deeper in the book of Exodus, when we look at Mount Sinai, the giving of the Ten Commandments occurred. This really is a wedding ceremony. It reflects God coming to his people and calling them to himself. I am calling you to be my people. I am calling you to be my bride. Then later on in the Bible we read the church becomes the bride of Christ. We read and see that God is wanting to have a relationship with HIS people.

This is the whole premise of the Old Testament starting in the Garden of Eden right through to the New Testament. To summarise the whole Bible, it says; I AM THE GOD WHO DELIVERS YOU! And how does God do this? He does it in Eden, He did it on the Ark, He did it in Babel, He did it out of Egypt, He did it out of the dessert to the promise land, and He did it with his Son Jesus. One day God will come down and deliver us and take us to be with Him in His Fathers house.

The entire premise and the entire Bible says that God wants to have a relationship with you. He wants to be apart of your marriage. Nothing more, nothing less. Marriage is not a structure, it's not a contract. Everyday we are in a relationship with God, there is no part-time or special occasions with God.

He is in every part of every hour of every day. Everyday you are married to Him, everyday you have an opportunity to be in a relationship with Him.

It's not healthy to view God as an accessory, yet we do this all the time. We use the term *'add'*. We *add* God to our marriage, we *add* God to our family, we *add* Him to our career, we *add* God to our finances. God is everything.

A Bride and Groom should have a mentality of adding themselves to God. They add their family to God, their finances to God and so forth. Everything flows from God. Lets look at what happened on Mount Sinai:

> *On the first day of the third month after the Israelites left Egypt on that very day they came to the Desert of Sinai. After they set out from Rephidim, they entered the Desert of Sinai, and Israel camped there in the desert in front of the mountain. Then Moses went up to God, and the Lord called to him from the mountain and said, 'This is what you are to say to the descendants of Jacob and what you are to tell the people of Israel: 'You yourselves have seen what I did to Egypt, and how I carried you on eagles' wings and* **brought you to myself.** *Now if you obey me fully and keep my*

> covenant, then out of all nations **you will be my treasured possession.** Although the whole earth is mine, you will be for me a kingdom of priests and a holy nation. These are the words you are to speak to the Israelites'.

Now every good husband knows how to talk to his beautiful wife. *'You are my treasured possession'.* Then the bride gives her consent, in Exodus verse 8 reads;

Moses then took the blood, (the cup) sprinkled it on the people and said 'This is the blood of the covenant that the LORD has made with you in accordance with all these words'.

We see this beautiful covenant taking place on Mount Sinai, where Moses takes the cup, the blood of the covenant and he says; *'take this cup, do it in remembrance that I have chosen you'*. This sounds so familiar doesn't it. Jesus Himself says in Luke 22:20 *'This cup is the new covenant in my blood, which is poured out for you'.*

Immediately the disciples would of had thoughts of Moses and Mount Sinai, the blood of the covenant. Their thoughts going straight back to the calling, starting back to when God called people to himself. Jesus said *'This is the blood of the covenant'.* Jesus was referring to, remember that my Father betrothed you, remember that you are mine. And how does He know? Because they have been sprinkled with the blood of the covenant. Then Jesus comes, He becomes the covenant and we take the cup in remembrance of Him.

Next we have the bridal gift. Who remembers their wedding gifts? How many toasters or gravy boats did you get? The bride is presented pure, washed clean, spotless of all flaws or sin. It's the same as a bride or groom today as they stand in front of a mirror getting ready for their big day. The Torah (the first five books of the Bible, the Law), has been seen as the gift of God. We have the word, now we have been given the Holy Spirit.

There is a Jewish term '*Mikvah*' which refers to a ritual bath which holds great spiritual significance. It is used for purification, renewal and transformation. A *Mikvah* can be described as a baptismal bath. It's a place to be spiritually cleansed, so the bride would go into a *Mikvah*.

In Exodus 19:10; *And the LORD said to Moses, 'Go to the people and consecrate them today and tomorrow. Have them wash their clothes, have them wash themselves'.* Another area we see people being cleansed today is through the waters of Baptism. Jesus himself was Baptised. He got Baptised in the Jordan river symbolic of a *Mikvah*. He was cleansed and purified, perfect and Holy. Then Jesus calls us to be Baptised. He calls us to be clean.

Why do we do this? Because its part of the wedding ceremony. It all starts with God. Baptism isn't just a ritual that we merely go through, its part of the wedding ceremony, its part of becoming His own, when we get washed and become cleansed and become new, symbolically we become pure.

Now it's the Grooms turn. In the Jewish culture the Bride waits for the Grooms return to finalise the wedding. Going back to Mount Sinai, Israel enters a waiting period before they go into the promise land. This waiting period also points forward to the messianic expectations of Jesus returning for His Bride. We see this played out in the parable of the Ten Virgins (Matthew 25:1-13), where five burnt their oil lamps really quickly, and then the other five trimmed their lamps and waited for the Bride to come. This is the picture Jesus paints for us on His return. Some marriages will start off fast and will live their life hard, and towards the end they are burnt out often ending in divorce.

But then there will be couples who will continue to push through the tough times, they will go little further, try a little harder, put in that extra effort in their christian walk. Couples now realise that this martial walk is no longer a sprint but rather worth the wait for Jesus' return.

Then we have the *'Chuppah'* (Hoppa), known as a canopy or covering that goes over the Bride and Groom during the wedding ceremony or marriage bed. We read of a cloud over Mount Sinai in Exodus chapter 19 reads; *On the morning of the third day there was thunder and lightning, with a thick cloud over the mountain.* Thus, symbolising his glory and presence to His people.

You see, if you and your spouse are planing to be married, you are called to *'prepare'*. We see this being played out today in the wrong ways, where men have their bucks nights often involving the best man, and other groomsmen becoming over intoxicated and engaging in acts for their very last time. We hear about brides-to-be having fancy hens nights, and again she will party with her bridesmaids til all hours of the morning. Celebrating like she is doomed and will never experience fellowship or take another sip of wine again. So they all party hard, only to wake up feeling miserable and hung over the next day. Its like they partied with Racheal but woke up with Leah…now life is hard! Your marriage has been designed for a purpose, God wants you to lay hands on the younger generation and pray for them, to help, to surround them with excellence and testimonies of your journeys through the tough stuff in marital life.

They are not getting enough mentoring or tools, young marriages are not getting enough knowledge and wisdom. What starts off beautiful can often end up a disaster. God has called us to rise up.

If you are preparing to be married you are called to look your best on your wedding day, living a life of Holiness. Wedding dresses have changed over the years, from the classic modest style to flamboyant and modern designs. A bride can wear white to black depending on her values, morals and beliefs. Then there are the flowers, the hair, the nails, and make-up. I was nervous on gaining any weight, I watched what I ate. Like most brides we focus of fitting into our dress. I had to stay ready, I was preparing myself for the big day. The value of a wedding dress is 'priceless'. God has clothed you with HIS Sons righteousness, He did it all for us, because He is the God who delivers you. The bridal dress was bought by the blood of Jesus. Jesus died, He rose again, He ascended to the Father, the Bible says that He has clothed us in HIS righteousness.

God says, one day we will be together and we will sit down and feast. Then we will celebrate the *'I AM, the God who delivered you'*. Our whole marital journey here on earth is a reminder that He is the God who delivered us. He is the God who set us free from our temptation, from our sin and wickedness which started in Eden, He is the God that has set us free. He is THE GREAT I AM.

The entire Bible from Genesis through to Revelations. God is in the garden who only wants a relationship with man. All He wants is to be close. Then if you turn to the back of the Bible, right over to the end of Revelations, there it is…we are together with Him. Are you ready? Are you a Bride in waiting, standing motionless in front of the mirror, not knowing what to expect. Are you preparing for your groom to come? Or are you caught up in the word full of other gods, other commitments and full of material distractions. Are your eyes fixed on Him? The one true love, the finisher and the perfecter of our faith, who is love, who gives love and offers His love to you throughout your covenant lives. And finally, when the happy Groom lifts his Bride up over the threshold into their new home, this signifying to ascend, or to 'rapture' (her) 'the Bride' up to her Groom. Building and planning takes an enormous amount of time. God has already laid out His blueprint for you mapped out in the Bible.

The room is electrified with anticipation. The shout of the guests is so powerful that it mimics the sounds of a storm crashing through the mountains. The celebration has come! The guests have arrived! The radiant bride steps forth to greet her husband. God is setting things up for the return of His Son. Believers' hearts are being stirred. The Bridegroom is coming soon to retrieve His Bride, the Church. Still, there are many lingering questions: When will these things happen? What can we expect? Are we in the end days? How can we be ready? What specific things does the Bible teach us about the Rapture and the events that follow? The image of Christ returning for his bride is so beautiful that it drives us to worship. Even more amazing is that this vision is about us. Those who follow Christ, who love and serve him, whom He has redeemed, we are the church, the bride of Christ!

Lord Jesus, prepare us for the day of your return. Your bride is preparing for her wedding day. Come, Lord; come quickly.
In your name we pray. Amen.

Day 3 Devotion questions
The Bride of Christ

The imagery and symbolism of marriage is applied to Christ and the body of believers known as the church. The church is comprised of those who have trusted in Jesus Christ as their personal Saviour and have received eternal life. Christ, the Bridegroom, has sacrificially and lovingly chosen the church to be His bride. Just as there was a betrothal period in Biblical times during which the bride and groom were separated until the wedding, so is the bride of Christ separate from her Bridegroom during the church age.

Her responsibility during the betrothal period is to be faithful to Him. At the rapture, the church will be united with the Bridegroom and the official 'wedding ceremony' will take place and, with it, the eternal union of Christ and His bride will be actualised.

How does the relationship between the church and Christ compare to an earthly marriage?

_____
_____
_____

Discussion

Discuss and share your thoughts on the following passages:

Ephesians 5:25-27, 2 Corinthians 11:2, Ephesians 5:24, Revelations 19:7-9, Revelations 21:1-2.

'Let us be glad and rejoice, and let us give honour to him. For the time has come for the wedding feast of the Lamb, and his bride has prepared herself'.

- Revelations 19:7

Jesus is coming back to take His followers, His Bride, back with Him.
Are you prepared to be the Bride of Christ?
If not, what is holding you back?

_____
_____
_____
_____
_____
_____
_____

Devotion day 4. Running the race

Read Hebrews 12:1-2: *'Therefore, since we are surrounded by such a great cloud of witnesses, let us throw off everything that hinders and the sin that so easily entangles. And let us run with perseverance the race marked out for us, fixing our eyes on Jesus, the pioneer and perfecter of faith. For the joy set before him he endured the cross, scorning its shame, and sat down at the right hand of the throne of God'.* Watching the Olympics, I am often captivated by the incredible human strength, perseverance, and dedication. The athletes didn't just show up and compete, hoping to do well. They have been training for years, making sacrifices and striving towards one goal. They want to finish well and win Gold!

In some ways, marriage can be like running an Olympic race. Marriage requires teamwork, endurance, and an unwavering focus on the goal. If one spouse stops running the race or shifts their focus, it can cause issues. The scripture from Hebrews beautifully parallels the journey of marriage. Like Olympic athletes, couples must prepare for their journey together, supporting and encouraging each other as they navigate the course. *'For this reason a man will leave his father and mother and be united to his wife, and the two will become one flesh'* (Ephesians 5:31).

Olympic athletes often rely on coaches, teammates, and family for support and encouragement. A healthy marriage must also survive on support and teamwork. In marriage, spouses should lift each other up, share burdens, and celebrate victories together. Having a community of friends who can support and pray for you will also be beneficial. That could even be one other couple, but don't fall into the trap of isolation. The path to Olympic gold is rarely smooth; it is marked by trials, setbacks, and challenges. Likewise, marriage can be challenging. Perseverance through difficult times can strengthen the bond in your relationship and deepen your relationship with God and each other.

As we observe the dedication of Olympic athletes, we should be inspired to run our marriage race with the same vigour and commitment. In marriage, as in athletics, success comes from dedication, teamwork, perseverance, and an unwavering focus on the ultimate goal.

'Fixing our eyes on Jesus, the author and perfecter of faith …' The race of marriage is really a race of faith. This is the part that so many couples forget. We try to maintain our marriage in our own power, and so often we fail because we don't realise that marriage is ultimately a spiritual relationship, between a man, a woman, and God. Not only does God call you to pledge lifelong commitment to each other, but He also gives you the strength to keep your vows, no matter what happens. When you fix your eyes on Jesus as you run the race of marriage, you realise your purpose is to serve Him and not seek your own fulfilment. When you and your spouse follow Him and draw closer to Him, you draw closer to each other. You recognise that there is much about marriage that is beyond your power; who has the ability, for example, to *'love your wife as Christ loves the church'* (Ephesians 5:25). Instead, it is God who is *'at work in you, both to will and to work for His good pleasure'* (Philippians 2:13). He will *'equip you in every good thing to do His will'* (Hebrews 13:21). In marriage there are seasons of trial and testing, when all you can think about is the long and painful road ahead. But God's Word gives us hope, and promises us the joy that can only be found when you know Christ as your Lord and Saviour. Psalm 126:5-6 reads, *'Those who sow in tears will reap with songs of joy. He who goes out weeping, carrying seed to sow, will return with songs of joy, carrying sheaves with him'*. In the distance race of marriage, it's important to lay aside anything that hinders your ability to hold true to your vow to remain committed to your spouse: to have and to hold, from this day forward, for better or for worse, in sickness and in health, till death do us part. Run with perseverance, you will have your good days and hard ones in your marital journey. The only way to see progress in your walk is to *'just keep swimming'*. Keep seeking God through daily prayer, praise, and reading His word on the days when you feel like it and the days when you don't. Today's emotions and feelings do not control us. Growth and maturity come in the hard times, not in the easy, when we refuse to give up and continue to seek Him! Fix our Eyes on Jesus, you need a goal or a destination. In our relationship with God, that vision board is the cross of Christ. As Christ followers, we model Jesus and lay down our lives in daily surrender to the purposes and plans of God. We know that Jesus has victory over sin and death through His death and resurrection and now sits at the right hand of God. Through His power, we can also have victory! Athletes often rely on coaches, teammates, and family for support and encouragement. A healthy marriage must also survive on support and teamwork. Don't run the race of marriage alone!

Day 4 Devotion questions
Running the Race

The Bible teachers us in 1 Corinthians 9:24 (CEV), It reads, 'Many runners enter a race, and only one of them wins the prize. So, run to win'. Life is like a race, and we are encouraged to run it well. Do your best to win the prize. The prize of eternal life is for everyone who receives Jesus Christ as Lord and Saviour.

Marriage is like the race of life. How well are you running?

_____
_____
_____
_____
_____

The Apostle Paul, in another of his letters in the Bible, puts it like this: 'I press on toward the goal for the prize of the upward call of God in Christ Jesus' (Philippians 3:14 NASB).

Athletes, not only nourish their body and recover well, but they also work hard to build endurance. They endure long runs, they do speed workouts, they lift weights, they stretch, they push through pain. They have sore muscles and tired lungs. Likewise in a marriage, we work hard to strengthen our faith to endure the race of faith. We ought to seek God daily in His Word and in prayer. We ought to seek fellowship among other believers and let our fellow church members encourage us in the faith. We must welcome correction and embrace trials. Personal discipline is essential if we are to keep our eyes focused on the prize - Jesus.

What does pressing on to reach the end of the race look like in your life?

_____
_____
_____

Do you feel your spouse is more advanced in their walk with God than you?

_____
_____
_____

DEVOTION DAY 5. KEYS TO A HAPPY MARRIAGE

Marriage is a gift from God, and it's also the most challenging relationship most people experience. Both husband and wife have to make a determined, diligent commitment to love each other, and that means submission and sacrifice. It's so important to understand this and to receive God's unconditional love for us if we want to really love our spouse. Without His love, we won't have the ability to give everything needed for marriage. I know about this from personal experience because when I married my husband, I was a mess! Because of the severe abuse I had endured from my previous marriage, I had feelings of being insecure, I felt emotionally damaged through condemnation and shame spoken over my life. So I had to push through the walls of my heart to trust my husband and submit to him the way God wanted me to. However, as I became more desperate to have peace in my life, I began to seriously pursue a personal relationship with Jesus and learnt how to study the Bible in areas that mattered to my heart the most. It's the best decision I ever made because it led to a healing journey that radically changed my life, added value and knowledge to our marriage, and bought a new outlook of ministry to peoples lives.

Love is the highest form of maturity. It often requires a selfless sacrifice. If we aren't willing to make some sort of sacrifice on our part in marriage, we probably don't love the other person at all. The kind of love people can give in and of themselves is so limited. It gives back in response to what someone has done (often out of a sense of obligation) and it is often used to manipulate others to gain control of them. But God's love is pure, selfless, and unconditional. He doesn't give us His mercy or favour only if we deserve it or try to earn it from Him through good works. No, God loves us because He IS love, it's who He is and what He does - Read 1 John 4:8.

When it comes to marriage, you must have God's love in your heart in order to truly love your spouse. When you do, you'll always have his/her best interest in mind and desire to serve and support them. You'll focus more on what you can do for your spouse than striving to make sure you get your way all the time.

Sacrifice is not always fun or easy, but when it's motivated by Godly love, it always brings greater peace and joy to your soul. It is a powerful investment in your marriage that will reap great rewards because God will work in both of your lives in amazing ways as you trust and obey Him.

I'm so thankful God helped me understand the benefits of godly submission and sacrifice in my marriage. I want to encourage you to give your heart and your marriage to God completely. These are the keys. Trust Him to give you the grace to love your spouse as He loves you. The blessings that will come as you diligently submit and sacrifice as God leads you to do so will far outweigh the growing pains you experience in the process! Regardless of the what's and why's, I believe the challenges in a relationship can all boil down to five key areas that I consider the be the pillars of a great marriage: respect, being a helper, unity, love, and, above all, communication. Let's take them one at a time starting with respect. Treat your significant other the way you would want to be treated.

- Listen and communicate openly, as understanding each other's love language connects you more deeply; invest in meaningful conversations and be each other's confidante.
- Communicate your needs and engage in active listening to truly understand each other; make it a habit to create a safe space for open dialogue.

- Embrace forgiveness and acceptance, understanding that imperfection is a part of human nature; offer patience and grace to your partner through the highs and lows.

'A simple 'I love you' means more than money'
— Frank Sinatra

'We're friends, too. We love each other, but we actually like each other—and that's an important distinction there. Love is passion and all of that stuff, but actually liking somebody and enjoying someone's company is something slightly different, and it lasts longer. So you can have both, and I think that's important. Be married to your best friend'.
— Sting

'I have someone who I can talk to about anything and someone who I care more about than I've cared about anybody'.
— George Clooney

Day 5 Devotion Questions
Keys to a Happy Marriage

Marriage is God's design, intended for companionship, love, and oneness. However, many couples struggle because they have not fully embraced what it means to be knitted together as one. What is the key? The book of Genesis 2:24 reads; 'Therefore a man shall leave his father and mother and be joined to his wife, and they shall become one flesh'.

What does 'oneness' in marriage mean to you?

_____
_____
_____
_____

What practical steps can you take to weave your lives together more deeply?

_____
_____
_____
_____

God desires to bless your marriage, but it requires intentional effort. Love is not automatic it must be nurtured, protected, and rekindled.

What steps will you take today to strengthen your marriage?

_____
_____
_____
_____
_____

Read Matthew 19:6; 'What God has joined together, let not man separate'. Who is at the centre of your marriage, your emotions, your circumstances, or Christ?

_____
_____
_____
_____
_____

> *'A soft answer turns away wrath, but a harsh word stirs up anger'.*
>
> — Proverbs 15:1

Identify one habit you need to stop that may be harming your spouse. Write it down and discuss how to replace it with a loving response.

_____
_____
_____
_____
_____

How can you address these challenges in a way that strengthens your marriage?

_____
_____
_____
_____
_____

Remember your looking for a positive outcome that will strengthen not weaken your relationship. Don't look for blame or past circumstances that could add fuel to the fire. Choose the right time, communicate the right tone, use the correct words. Grow together in love.

Would you say that you love each other more now than earlier in your marriage?

_____
_____
_____
_____

How happy are you praying as a couple? What things can you change to make prayer more enjoyable?

_____
_____
_____
_____

Pause and Pray

'LORD BLESS OUR MARRIAGE. HELP US TO APPROACH OUR MARRIAGE WITH RESPECT AND HONOUR FOR OUR UNION, FOR YOU BROUGHT US TOGETHER. GIVE US A STRONGER HEART FOR EACH OTHER, AND HELP US TO UNDERSTAND EACH OTHERS NEEDS, THAT WE WILL BE A BLESSING. FOR WE KNOW, WHEN WE BLESS EACH OTHER, WE ARE BLESSING YOUR HEART AS WELL AND BRINGING GLORY TO YOUR NAME'.

IN JESUS NAME - AMEN.

Chapter Nine
Honey we need to talk

'Let your conversation be always full of grace, seasoned with salt, so that you may know how to answer everyone'.

- Colossians 4:6 NIV

Devotion day 1

The day you married, is the same day you made incredible promises. Your spouse became your lawful wedded husband/wife from this day forward, to have and to hold, for better or worse, for richer or poorer, in sickness and in health, till death do you part. Yet, what about the vow to COMMUNICATE! We've heard them all so many times, in the movies, on television and of course at weddings, that we can recite them off by heart. Yet the hardest thing to live with is the effective art of communicating between one another?

Most of us don't realise that there is no legal reason to include these canonical words at a wedding ceremony. However, they have become part of the marriage performance. There is something touching about the many generations after generations of people saying the traditional wedding vow. But do they actually mean? These basic marriage vows, which are actually known as 'consent' in the christian ceremony, look simple, don't they? Communicating through each one throughout our marital walk is much more difficult. These simple wedding vows contain a world of 'meaning'. So, what are wedding vows? More importantly what is true meaning of marriage vows?

I take thee to be my wedded wife/husband is about free will. This isn't a forced marriage. You've selected this person. This voluntary decision establishes personal responsibility for your choice.

'Wedded' means connected, attached, united, joined, yoked. So the phrase 'I take thee to be my wedded wife (husband)' is really saying: 'I choose you as my teammate! I freely unite myself to you for life'.

To have and to hold from this day forward - is a property rights legal phrase that defines 'the extent of the interest that is granted or conveyed and the conditions affecting it'. But as part of the traditional marriage vows, this isn't a statement of ownership, it refers to belonging together.

For better, for worse, for richer, for poorer, in sickness and in health - This portion of the traditional marriage vows is a promise to stay faithful and committed no matter what happens. The book of 1 Corinthians 7:28 says, *'Those who marry will have worldly troubles'*. Life will have its ups and downs, good times and hard times. But traveling this journey together as husband and wife is what grows and deepens your love for each other.

To love and to cherish - Love means you will sacrifice, you'll give up something highly valued for the sake of someone else considered to have great value. Cherish means to recognise your spouse's incredible value as a human being, as a child of God and as the one person you've chosen to spend your life with.

Til death us do part - The phrase *'until death do us part'* means you're making a lifelong commitment, that death should be the only thing that dissolves the marriage bond. This vow was written by God in Matthew 19:4-6. *'Have you not read that he who created them from the beginning made them male and female, and said, 'Therefore a man shall leave his father and his mother and hold fast to his wife, and the two shall* *become one flesh'? So they are no longer two but one flesh. What therefore God has joined together, let not man separate'.*

As you consider or revisit these promises, you'll understand why traditional marriage vows have endured. Communicating these vows before God, and keeping them, is deeply meaningful and is worth any effort involved. Remember each vow looks different for everyone. Have your words ever become tangled and you have found yourself in a mess of words? I know mine have more times than I care to admit. The way we communicate, from body language and tone can shape our entire day. The most natural form of communication. When you ask, 'How was your day, honey'? the typical comments that follow would land under this heading of 'small talk'. However, these conversations are still important to your marriage. They establish a simple connection between you and your spouse that doesn't require exhausting emotional vulnerability. While intimacy requires vulnerability we can't be in a state of deep, emotional intimacy every moment of our relationship. We'd wear ourselves out! Other conversations can be more serious when our spouse has hurt or disappointed us, for instance, or we disagree on something critical. They can be talks that happen in the midst of deep grief, anger, or confusion when we've lost a job, or we're dealing with sickness.

Conversations connected to challenges can help us to grow, both as individuals and as a couple. They can expose our blind spots or lead us to make important and necessary changes in our lives. Thankfully God's Word has so much to say about how we use our words both for good and for evil. And it can really help us to learn what to say, how best to say it, and when we should just say nothing at all. Proverbs 16:24, says, 'Gracious words are a honeycomb, sweet to the soul and healing to the bones'. I love to drill down deep and learn the original Hebrew or Greek meaning of the words that are in the verses. I also like to just sit back and go, 'Hmm, why did God use honey to talk about our words being sweet? I wonder what makes honey sweet'. I didn't have to look far for my answer. Our local garden and hardware store often gets guest speakers in during the school holidays. A bee keeper was displaying his bees and talking about the environment. Filled with curiosity, I listened about his honey-making friends. He told me that there are two things that are so crucial that will make honey sweet and light with a delicate and delicious taste rather than dark and bitter with a lingering aftertaste that's quite unpleasant.

The first thing is, he said, *'that you need to be careful what the bees drink in. You want them to drink in the nectar from clover* rather than other flowers because clover makes the sweetest and lightest honey. You need to make sure you put that beehive near a patch of clover'. The second thing he said is *'that you want to place your beehive in a location where the sun will hit it first thing in the morning, warming the bees up so they get to work, go out and find that clover, and they make that sweet, delicious honey'*. I said to him, *'So, are you telling me that the sweetness or bitterness of honey is determined by what the bee drinks in and the amount of time it spends in the sun'?* The bee keeper replied, *'That's exactly it'*. I thought, 'Well, I think I've got my answer'. Perhaps it's also true that the sweetness or bitterness of our words will be directly determined by what we drink in and the amount of time that we spend each day in the *Son*. And I don't mean S-U-N. I mean S-O-N. May we all make it our aim to use our words in a way that is sweet, in a way that they bless and not badger, that they encourage, not embitter, that they are used in a way to praise rather than as a method to pounce.

So drink in what is good, spend time early in the *Son,* so that you too can have speech that is gracious and sweet.

Day 1 Devotion questions Honey we

NEED TO TALK

The first time a bride and groom officially communicate under a covenant is at the wedding ceremony. Its at this pivotal moment where you communicate your vows and understand they are for life!

How and when did you fall in love? What caught your attention?

_____
_____
_____
_____
_____
_____

What do you most admire about each other?

_____
_____
_____
_____
_____
_____

What do you hope for your future together?

_____
_____
_____
_____

What do you love most about them?

_____
_____
_____
_____

Just for fun, if you were to re-write your wedding vows today, what would you write? Write your wedding vows. Have fun with this, share amongst yourselves.

(Example; I promise to have and to hold, to leave the toilet set up, for better or for worse, to shop for richer and poorer, and to never replace the rubbish bag, but to always look after you when you have the man flu till death do us part...)

_____
_____
_____
_____
_____
_____
_____

Devotion day 2. Money talks

Money is something that's with us every day. It's saved, it's spent, it's scrounged, it's squeezed. People will do anything for money, but it makes you think how better to find God. Our loving Heavenly Father. God is our solid rock instead of money, because God values you more than any amount of money. (God loves you for eternity. When you die, your money is gone).

> *'No one can serve two masters, for either he will hate the one and love the other, or he will be devoted to the one and despise the other. You cannot serve God and money'*
>
> - Matthew 6:24

Money and marriage is a topic that intimidates most couples. The good news is you don't have to be a Wall Street broker or a Certified Financial Planner to manage your money wisely. God has much to say about money and our use of it in His Word. He has a financial plan that never fails regardless of how much you make or how much you owe. The focus of this plan is not on your money but on your heart. Its success is dependent on faith, not on a balance sheet. The reason so many of us get into financial trouble is because we fail to *communicate* with each other, understand and obey God's financial plan. When we put money where God should be in our lives, we end up loving money and trying to use God instead of loving God and letting Him use our money. God is the Master, money is the servant. This is always true in God's economy. There are only three things we can do with money: 1) Spend, 2) Save, and 3) Share. The vast majority of people manage money in this order. In this order, the first priority is 'me'. *I* spend money on what *I* want and what *I* need. Notice the second priority is also 'me'. If there is anything left over *I* might save some. God, then, is left in third place with the leftovers. And let's be honest, there are rarely any leftovers when we manage money this way. His plan requires faith. The key to His strategy is not to make more but to give more.

> *In all things I have shown you that by working hard in this way we must help the weak and remember the words of the Lord Jesus how He Himself said, 'It is more blessed to give than to receive,*
>
> - Acts 20:35

When we give God the first portion of our money, He will manage the rest. This requires tremendous faith, but He is faithful! I encourage you to follow God's money management plan for the next two months and see what happens. Make your first 10% out to God and His Kingdom. Make the second to savings (even if it is just a small amount). Make your third payment to debt (even if it is only a small amount). Then pay whatever taxes and bills you have to pay and live on what is left over. This plan may not make sense on paper, but you must believe that since God gives you eternal life through Christ, He can also give you anything you need in this life. The key is effective communication. God will fill your boat and break your nets with overwhelming blessings! Is money an issue in your marriage? Many marriages have been ripped apart over riches. Many newly married couples don't know how to handle their finances in a way that honours God. I don't want you to be one of them. I don't want you to be caught off guard.

The most important thing I can tell you is that money isn't the problem. Our hearts are. Your financial life is always determined more by the desires of your heart than by the size of your income. To the degree that you ask money to provide for you what it was never meant to provide, to that degree you will find it very hard to be careful and disciplined in your use of money. Money can't buy you a satisfied heart, money can't buy you peace and happiness, and money can't buy you a reason to get up in the morning. Money isn't meant to be your source of comfort when you are hurting or of hope when you are feeling discouraged. Money can't and was never intended to give you life. To ask money to do any of those things will always lead to money troubles. We all have greedy tendencies. Every married couple has a heart that can cling to money more than Christ. It is the *love* of money that is the root of all kinds of evil. You can be greedy with $10,000 or $10.00.

You might love to spend money to get stuff. Your love for money might manifest itself in a pile of possessions or a catalogue of experiences. You love to keep money in the bank for security. Whether you save it, spend it, or invest it, you can still be infected with idolatry. Jesus said that we cannot serve both God and money (Matthew 6:24). We cannot serve two masters. You must decide who you will serve. Greed and God's glory don't go together. Will it command your desires? Will you love it? or will you love Jesus? A budget is a projection of how you plan to spend your income. Sit down together as a couple and chart out how much money to spend. You can also do this for birthdays, special occasions, and holidays. See money as a means to an end, not an end in itself.

Day 2 Devotion questions
Money Talks

Addressing the issue of money and understanding money problems doesn't begin with money and budget information; it begins with surrender.

You and I will never use money the way it was meant to be used, and we will never break disastrous money habits if we are not living in light of the fact that life is not about us. The world wasn't first created to be a vehicle for realising our personal definition of happiness. Money wasn't created for the sole purpose of bringing into our lives all the things we crave.

If we don't start with surrender, even if we're not in debt, we will use money in a way that God never intended. In this way maybe many of us have more money problems than we realise. We think we're okay because we are able to pay the price of our pleasures, but we're not okay, because what shapes our money matters is a spirit of ownership rather than a spirit of surrender.

The first step in money sanity is surrendering to the glory of one greater than you. Carefully read through the following questions and openly discuss with your spouse your personal views on God and money.

- Is money my master, or is God?
- Is money my security, or is God?
- Is money my treasure, or is my treasure eternal?
- Am I fulfilling my responsibilities?
- Is money mine, or is it God's?
- Am I helping the needy?
- Am I guarding my integrity?
- Am I at peace?
- Am I grateful? Does your money, car, or house belong to you, or to God?
- Am I gambling my money away on internet games or t.v subscriptions.

'The earth is the Lord's, and everything in it, the world, and all who live in it'
- Psalm 24:1

Devotion day 3. Family communication

Communication within your family is extremely important because it enables members to express their needs, wants, and concerns to each other. Open and honest communication creates a healthy atmosphere that allows family members to express their differences as well as love and admiration for one another. It is through communication that family members are able to resolve the unavoidable problems that arise in all families, that's right *all* families. Just as effective communication is found in strong, healthy marriages and families, poor communication is usually found in unhealthy family relationships. Many of us have difficult family members and sometimes it feels so hard to love them how we know God wants us to. Some couples get married into a family circle where a close relative battles addictions. Deep down you and your spouse love them and you know God loves them and wants to see them healed more than you do. Feelings of grief and angry hinder your relationship as you watch them continually make poor life choices. Family burdens and their past can wear you down as a couple. Then there are families burdened by generational curses God wants to fix. Maybe those curses have already been verbally broken over your life. But there's a practical side to breaking generational curses that involve fixing relationships. Uniting both sides of the families can be difficult and at times awkward.

Marriage and family therapists often report that poor communication is a common complaint of families who are having difficulties. Poor communication is unclear and indirect. It can lead to numerous family problems, including excessive repetitive family conflict, ineffective problem solving, lack of intimacy, and weak emotional bonding.

Poor communication such as abusive language delivered through anger or rage is also associated with an increased risk of divorce and marital separation, and behavioural problems in children. These behaviours, if not rectified can have a significant impact on how the next generation views and acts in his or her future relationships. Have you ever seen a family where the father has a problem with uncontrollable anger and seen his son act and communicate within a similar way. It's like his father 'handed it' to him, maybe the grandfather had the same problem? Or have you noticed that not only do you suffer from something such as persistent irrational fears or depression, but your mother and her father also suffered from it as well? There are many people today who are living under bondage that the sins of their forefathers has brought them under. What are you communicating to each other and to your children? The influence of your vow *'to have and to hold'* or something else? Is there someone in your family you can love better? Is there a relationship that you need to mend? Ask God to show you how to love them as He does. The Bible reminds us, *'A house is built by wisdom.'* (Proverbs 24:3 NLT). The storms of life will test whether or not you've done a good job with your family. And an important key to succeeding at home is communication. So, ask yourself these four questions:

1. How well do you communicate with the people you love? You may unwittingly have adopted a style that doesn't work well for you. For example: do you retaliate? That has a degrading effect. Do you dominate? That has an intimidating effect. Do you isolate? That has a frustrating effect. Or do you co-operate? That has an encouraging effect. If you're in the habit of using any communication style other than a co-operative one, you must work to change it if you want to build a good relationship with your family.

2. Have you identified your communication killers? The internet, iPhones, and TV are among the chief culprits. Would it surprise you to know the average couple spends less than an hour a week in meaningful conversation, and approximately five hours a day watching television and playing on thier iPhones?

3. Do you encourage everyone to speak their mind? And when they do speak freely do you criticise, pout, or retaliate? Differences of opinion can be healthy. The Bible says, '*Iron sharpens iron*'. (Proverbs 27:17) Handled respectfully, different opinions can make things better for everyone.

4. Do you think creatively? Do you spend time together as a family? Do you call your spouse during the day and try to meet sometimes for lunch? Do you drive your kids to school or sports activities so you can talk to them? Communication can happen anywhere, but it only happens when you make it a priority.

Day 3 Devotion questions
Family communication

Communication issues can be one of the deadliest but unrealised problems a family will face. We tend to focus just on the major fights or what happens when it all comes to a head. However, if our communication as a family was addressed earlier on, it might even help prevent those major conflict points from occurring.

The goal isn't to avoid conflict but to build healthy communication systems that allow your family to communicate well through all stages. Simple tools like the questions you ask as a family can help you build a regular routine and clear communication standards.

How have you felt listened to and valued?
_____
_____
_____
_____

What words of encouragement do you need to hear?

_____
_____
_____
_____

What does it look like to bring out the best in each other?

_____
_____
_____
_____

How do you feel about understanding each other's unique ways of communication?

_____
_____
_____
_____
_____
_____

How have you been practicing building/rebuilding trust?

_____
_____
_____
_____

How have you been practicing active listening and asking clarifying questions?

_____
_____
_____
_____

Are past hurts still impacting how you communicate?

_____
_____
_____

Have you held each other accountable for respectful and intentional communication?

_____
_____
_____
_____

Are there any promises or expectations that are not being followed through. Write/discuss any areas that need to be addressed.

_____
_____
_____
_____
_____

Remember, to improve communication in a marriage and family environment, ask open-ended questions about feelings, goals, and needs, covering topics like finances, responsibilities, dreams, and how to support each other. Focus on building a stronger environment, through open dialogue about what makes each person feel loved and appreciated, and what the future looks like together.

PAUSE AND PRAY

'LORD BLESS OUR MARRIAGE. CLEANSE OUR HEARTS FROM BITTERNESS AND REPLACE IT WITH COMPASSION, PATIENCE, AND LOVE. DRAW US TOGETHER AS WE TALK, UNIFYING US IN YOUR WISDOM AND GRACE. MAY YOUR LOVE SEASON OUR SPEECH, AND YOUR MERCY GUIDE OUR HEARTS. IN JESUS NAME - AMEN

Devotion day 4. Raising Tomorrows Bride and Groom.

Raising Godly kids in an ungodly world is not impossible. You and your children were born for such a time as this, as well as understanding God's heart. Married and now raising kids can feel impossible. Everywhere we turn in our culture, on television, in movies, and now through sexual education in secondary schools, our kids are being told to embrace unbiblical principals and to make their own personal choice. If there was an amount of money you could pay up front to get Godly children, parents would pay it! The biggest challenge and probably the one thing Christian parents worry about the most would have to be that their children love God their whole lives and make Godly decisions. Many people tell us how amazing our child is and ask us, 'How did you parent your son well'? Can I tell you that if you are looking for an easy answer to this question, there isn't one. Effective parenting involves a lot of hard work, knowing what God's Word says about parenting and total, utter reliance on the Holy Spirit to guide you. It also involves us to step aside and allow God to do His job. Some parenting styles include: Authoritative, Authoritarian, Permissive, Helicopter, Tiger mum, Hummingbird, Attachment, Free-range. We can learn a little something about ourselves and how we parent by thinking about the ideologies that underlie these titles. If you are like most people, you might recognise elements of each category that characterise your own parenting approach.

Our priority as parents is to truly understand the depth of love God has for us. It is only out of this understanding that we can parent our child. Before anything else, you must know you are loved unconditionally by God. Our self-worth must rest on God's never failing, never ceasing love for us. It is from this position of confidence in being God's beloved child first, that we can give unconditional love to our family. Maintain a great Marriage! One of the most destructive forces in our culture is the breakdown of the Biblical family structure. As parents, we must protect our families from division. It is critical for us to foster unity in the home. This means laying aside our own agendas for the most important work of building a great marriage. Marriage won't work unless you put your marriage and your spouse first. Great marriages make great families. Stability in your marriage will directly affect your ability to parent. Much of the security that your child/ren feels will come from the knowledge that their Mum and Dad love each other and that their relationship is a priority in the family. Parents often lose sight of the fact that when a child/ren enters their family, they enter an already established social structure. Many parents act as if the marriage union was only a preliminary relationship to nest-building rather than perceiving it as an ongoing priority relationship throughout the child-rearing years that demands prioritisation.

Cultivate a desire for Jesus in your children. Set the example! I have heard so many parents admit to sending their children to a Christian school in the hope that they would become a Christian. Seriously nothing could be further from the truth. Prior to the age of 11, children cannot process abstract concepts, so when it comes to Christian spirituality, words mean very little. They believe what they see demonstrated and they comprehend what they observe predominately in their parents. Be authentic in your faith. What they see you do and say at church, make sure you do and say at home. They are watching us as parents in everything we do. You are raising a future husband or future wife for someone's else's child.

Everyone has an opinion on how to parent and families are bombarded with suggestions. The Bible is and always will be the best place to understand how to parent. Dualism is a two-world perspective: biblical and secular. It essentially combines a secular worldview on parenting with a Biblical worldview. Many Christian families mix the two or take 'so-called' experts' advice. If anyone claims to be an expert, they haven't parented for long enough! Look for good parenting fruit in the lives of people from whom you receive parenting advice.

A Biblically-based home is one that understands that God's Word is <u>truth</u>. As your children grow, so does their need to understand the world around them. It is your job to show them the world from the perspective of God's Word. Discipline gets a terrible rap in our society, however, it is essential to help our children understand Godly authority. Critical to discipline is listening to the Holy Spirit to get the balance right. Excessive, harsh authority with no grace leads to rebellion. Child-centered overindulgences and tolerance to disobedience also lead to rebellion. Critical to discipline is listening to the Holy Spirit to get the balance right. Make it your aim to never correct your children in anger or humiliate them. Children need correction, however, they need this done from a position of relationship. You must maintain a relationship of trust and fairness so that correction will be received. Don't ever let the sun go down on your anger. The process of 'discipling' and correcting literally comes from the word '<u>disciple</u>'. As such, the discipline process involves training, correction, restoration, and affirmation. Training is teaching self-discipline so that a child can eventually establish it as a life practice. Boundaries are essential as the starting point for discipling. Establish clear, age-appropriate boundaries and remember to communicate. God has not left us alone as parents in the journey to raise Godly children. Remember the Holy Spirit and God's Word will never fail to show us the way. May God bless you as you raise the next generation of Bride and Grooms, amazing God loving children! Proverbs 22:6 addresses the subject of discipline, how a parent should correct a child. Most English translations read very closely to the NIV. I learned it as *'Train a child in the way he should go, and when he is old he will not depart from it'*. It says something slightly different in Hebrews: *'Train a child in **his** way, and when he is old he will not depart from it'*. The meaning is mostly the same parents should discipline children but it comes out a bit differently in Hebrews. This proverb is not saying that if you raise your children to be godly and wise (*'the way they should go'*) then you are guaranteed a good outcome. Rather, this proverb states that raising a child in **his** way means that he/she will stay that way (again, principles, not promises). Put another way, since Genesis 3 every human heart has bent toward evil. We are selfish, prideful, and sinful, every one of us. If we allow a child to continue on that path of selfishness and sin (pursuing 'his or her way'), then that's most likely how they will live their whole lives. The stakes are high, very high, so be encouraged, parents, and ask God for His wisdom, grace, and steadfastness while you lovingly correct your children. God's discipline for us is an example of how a good parent will discipline a child (Deuteronomy 8:5). God corrects us for our own good. He wants us to 'share in His Holiness' (Hebrews 12:10).

We often confuse Godliness with good behaviour. But raising Godly children is not the same as raising *'good'* children. Godliness is about the heart. It's about nurturing a relationship with God, not just policing behaviour. A child can appear respectful on the outside but be lost and uncertain on the inside. True godliness flows from knowing God. And that can't be forced or faked. It has to be cultivated through love, example, and honest conversation.

Raising Godly children is not for the faint of heart. You no doubt know of children who were raised in the faith and yet fell away. Sadly, this is not as rare as you would think. Yet for many dads who grieve for their prodigal sons or daughters, let's agree on one thing: the story isn't over yet. There is hope. God isn't finished with you or your children.

Day 4 Devotion questions
Raising tomorrows Bride and Groom

Read John 10:10. God's way of life is the abundant life and this life gives parents the opportunity to watch their children grow up making good decisions and avoiding decisions they may later regret. Learning how to live out these traits in our parenting gives our children a model for living out His abundant life.

What is the Biblical principle of parenting?

_____
_____
_____
_____
_____

The Bible says a lot about Christian parenting, emphasising the importance of raising children in a way that honours God. Key principles include recognising children as a blessing from God, diligently teaching them Scripture, modelling a godly life, and providing for their needs. Parenting children God's way is about following His guidance and not relying on secular methods or personal preferences. Parents are called to represent God in the home, reflecting His character and relying on His grace and strength.

Describe God's way of parenting?

_____
_____
_____
_____
_____

Think of some attainable spiritual goals that you can motivate your children to achieve.

_____
_____
_____
_____
_____
_____

Discuss with your spouse and consider teaching your child/ren the following five principles listed.

1. **Faith** - Teach your child/ren about God's love and the importance of faith in their lives. Help them understand the teachings of the Bible and how to apply them in their daily lives.

2. **Compassion** - Encourage your child/ren to show kindness and compassion towards others, just as Jesus did. Teach them to empathise with those who are less fortunate and to help those in need.

3. **Forgiveness** - Teach your child/ren the power of forgiveness, both in seeking forgiveness from others and in forgiving those who have wronged them. Help them understand that forgiveness is an essential part of living a Christian life.

4. **Integrity** - Teach your child/ren the value of honesty and integrity. Encourage them to always speak the truth and to do what is right, even when it is difficult.

5. **Humility** - Help your child/ren develop a sense of humility, recognising that they are not perfect and need God's grace in their lives. Teach them to be humble in their actions and words.

Encourage your child/ren to be confident! Teach them to embrace their strengths and weaknesses, knowing that God's grace is sufficient in their weakness. Encouraging your child/ren to be confident means helping them believe in themselves and also teaching them to stay strong in their faith, even when things get tough. By nurturing their confidence in God and themselves, you empower them to live boldly and make a positive impact on the world around them. You are raising a future Bride and Groom. Keep up the good work!

Pause and Pray

'LORD BLESS OUR MARRIAGE. THANK YOU FOR ALL THE PRECIOUS CHILDREN IN THIS WORLD. WE PRAY YOU WOULD HELP US DO ALL WE CAN TO PROTECT AND GIVE THEM THE START IN LIFE THEY DESERVE.
IN JESUS NAME - AMEN

Devotion day 5. Talking Vs. Listening

Our conversations don't need to be filled with anger, rage, slander, lies, or foul language (Read Colossians 3:8). Instead, as we follow Jesus and learn to take His attitude toward our spouse, we show grace for each other's faults. Husband's and wive's have their troubles. She says to him, *'If I've told you once, I've told you 100 times'.* He's not really listening to her. His mind is on something else. Active listening requires deliberate purpose, focus and attention. It's more than just paying attention. Can you listen without interrupting? It's actually very hard to do. We want to offer our own opinion, butt in and override the conversation and we all want to be heard. Try it sometime and you'll discover what I mean. Being a good listener takes discipline and a lot of hard work.

But do people really listen? Does a Bride and Groom really listen to each when speaking their vows to each other? We hear them, but are we really taking in what they mean? Maybe we hear only what we want to hear. Listening is so basic that we take it for granted. Others appear to be listening to you, but their minds are miles away somewhere else. This problem is everywhere. Social networking is all about talking and telling, and not about listening. But listening effectively bridges the gap between you and your spouse. The good listener appreciates you as you are, accepts your feelings as valid, even though you may have different opinions.

We must learn to suspend our own interests to focus on the other person, even for a while. No judging only an act of kindness by you keeping quiet. Giving advice is not the best. If I said, *'Well, if I were you I would do this'*, what I'm really saying is, 'Stop bothering me with your whining and *do something about it'*. Hardly a helpful way to think. Some spouse's are hard to live with, but that doesn't mean you stop listening to them. James 1:19 reads, *'Everyone should be quick to listen and slow to speak'.* God has created us to be relational people. We have an inner need to be linked with others, friends, family, and the community. But these relationships have to be worked at through being a good listener, to listen with love and care. Proverbs 18:2 says, *'A fool finds no pleasure in understanding, but delights in airing his own opinions'*. By listening, we put aside our own agenda, take a break from what we're doing, and give our full attention to the other spouse. It shows you really do care, that it's worth your time, and in turn, strengthens your relationship. It says, I have respect for you because I might learn something new for myself, to help my life. Therefore, out of respect for you, I will listen carefully. When will we learn that God knows the way ahead better than we do? The Bible has so much to say about that. If we pray, we think it's all about ourselves and what we want, a 'one-way' conversation. But we don't listen to God's response, and we miss out on so much. Psalm 46:10, says *'Be still and know that I am God'* —*'be still'* meaning hush and listen.

Listening to God isn't always easy. We have our expectations for what we think He may sound like, and when those expectations aren't met, we may question whether we actually heard God's voice. With all the voices shouting at us, social media, television, friends, family or even the messages we hear in church, how can we be sure that we are hearing God's voice rather than our own thoughts or the devil's lies? Many times, his voice is a whisper. You can only hear it if you listen hard enough. How do you listen to God's voice?

Elijah illustrates this for us in 1 Kings verse19, where he stood on a mountain and heard God speak to him. Elijah could have been fooled. What many people thought was, the Lord's voice, an incredible show of God's power, such as a natural disaster or a loud voice raining down from heaven, but he continued to listen, and instead, God's voice came to him as a whisper.

If Elijah wasn't listening, he may have missed it. God can, and often does, speak using a loud voice. He often spoke this way in the Bible and continues to speak to us using a loud voice today. God's shout isn't difficult to hear, but the real challenge is to listen to it. When a thought or a feeling stands out, or when you feel that God is trying to get your attention, tune into it. If you hear a shout from the Lord, this is an opportunity to ask questions and discern what God is trying to say to you.

The book of Proverbs repeatedly alludes to the value of using gentle words coated with pleasantness and sweetness when we speak. It does not refer to flattery but plainly speaking the truth with gentleness and love as this can actually extinguish the fire of anger. In an argument or moments of animosity if we learn the power of gentle words, it can completely change the atmosphere and put out the heat.

Proverbs also mentions that *'sweetness of lips increases learning'*. That means people are better able to receive what is being said when presented in a gentle manner rather than in a harsh and arrogant way. The Bible also refers to our words (likened to a honeycomb) blessing the receiver or hearer, impacting their hearts.

There is nothing more annoying than people not listening to your conversation, you know what it's like. You have a great story to tell your friend about a trip you went on last holidays. You want to share all the details, only to find they start off, Oh yes. I had a holiday last year too…And before you know it, it's all about them.

I'm afraid it happens all the time. Don't start off with your stories of ill health, because you're sure to hear about their sickness' details. It's almost as if they can't listen for two minutes. There may be a simple reason, are they getting deaf and actually can't hear you? Probably the real reason is they are too self-absorbed. In some cases, people are so wrapped-up in their own lives and concerns that they just don't want to listen to you, or anyone else. With these people, it can be very difficult to get them to listen to you. About the only way is to put the subject in terms of how it will affect them. And that can be tricky, and annoying. I'm talking about *listening skills,* something we don't talk a lot about, probably because we're too busy talking. Have you got the gift of really listening to others? It seems to me that talking can seem far more useful and attractive than listening, and so people will seek to talk rather than listen. When I talk, I am in control, and can steer the conversation any way that I choose.

You are a 'team', 'you are one' and 'you're in this together'. For better for worse, For richer for poorer, In sickness and in health, Til death do you part! *'You should be quick to listen and slow to speak.'* (James 1:19 CEV). In order to build good relationships, you must become a good listener. And in order to be a good listener, you must do these:

1. **Listen** without interrupting. Even when you know more than the person talking to you! Respect them enough to value what they say and listen attentively until they're finished.

2. **Try to understand** their point of view, feelings, thinking, and needs. In other words, listen to understand. Good listening is hearing what people actually think, mean, or feel, not what you imagine they should think, mean, or feel. Instead of guessing, politely ask, 'Am I understanding you correctly? Do you mean…? Are you feeling…?' Don't assume, verify.

3. **Avoid rushing to conclusions.** Listen without judging. If what they say doesn't quite add up, keep listening. *'He who answers a matter before he hears it, it is folly and shame to him.'* (Proverbs 18:13 NKJV) When you hear more, it may make sense.

4. **Refrain** from putting them on the defensive. Listen without correcting, countering, or devaluing. Saying, *'That's not the way it was,'* or *'What did you expect?'* or *'You're just being silly and too sensitive'* breaks real communication.

5. **Accept** their perceptions and feelings as valid expressions of a valued person. Validate the speaker. By saying, *'If I understand you correctly, you're thinking... feeling... am I right?'* Ask them to help you get on the same page with them. Saying, *'Given what you have told me, I can see why you would feel that way,'* will increase their willingness to consider your thoughts and accept the solutions you offer. If we want to make listening and learning one of our strengths, we need to identify how we currently listen to others. According to one theory, there are 4 different types of listeners:

1. **Non-listeners** – They don't listen to what you are saying. Instead they prefer hearing themselves talk.

2. **Marginal listeners** – Impatient to listen to the main ideas, marginal listeners pay superficial attention, and are interested only in the bottom line.

3. **Pretend listeners** – This listener type listens to your words, but doesn't hear the feelings you're conveying with your words. The pretend listeners observe your character, judge what you say and then decide on their response.

4. **Active listeners** – Active listeners pay absolute attention to what you are saying and to what you are communicating nonverbally. They do not interrupt and they ignore everything and everyone else around them.

It takes work to be an active listener. It takes focus, depth, self-control, and care. Basically, it takes a willingness to want to know. Jesus stopped and listened. You may never realise how much people need you to listen to them to be an active listener with care and compassion. When we listen, we invite another person to exist. For example: a mother who switches off the vacuum cleaner to listen to her child, a customer who stops to say *How are you*? to a sales clerk. Each of these is acknowledging someone's personhood. What prevents you from noticing the needs of others or listening well? How can you become a better listener?

Day 5. Devotion questions
Talking Vs. Listening

There's no magic formula for discerning God's voice. We learn to recognise His voice the way we recognise any voices of those close to us: by knowing Him. When we know Him, we can tell if what we're feeling led to do is from Him or not. I've heard His voice audibly. I can feel His direction and sense His presence when I seek Him. Here are five questions to determine if what you're hearing is from God.

Do you line up scripture with what you hear?
_____
_____
_____
_____

God will never tell us to do something contrary to His Word. But unless we know Scripture, we won't be able to discern whether what we hear is consistent with the Word. We know the will of God when we read and pray the Word of God. Get a journal, and start recording the verses you study and some of your personal experiences as you read Gods Word.

Is what you're hearing consistent with Gods character? Write down your understanding of Gods character.

_____
_____
_____
_____
_____

God's Word also provides rich information regarding His character. Just as God always speaks in accordance with His Word, He speaks in accordance with His character. God will not say anything inconsistent with who He is. The longer we know Him and the more we experience Him personally, the more we learn about His character. How would you describe yourself. Are you a talker or a listener?

_____
_____
_____
_____
_____

Is what you're hearing confirmed through messages at church or your community? Briefly explain your confirmation.

_____
_____
_____
_____
_____
_____

When God speaks to me about a particular issue, I cannot escape it. Around every corner, there's a sermon, Bible study lesson, speaker, or conversation with a friend that's consistent with what I've been hearing from God in my time alone with Him. Listen for His voice, and then look for the message to be confirmed by other trustworthy voices.

Is what you're hearing pleasing to God? What influences you?

_____
_____
_____
_____

The voice many people hear above God's is the voice of their own hurt, pain, disappointment, upbringing, bad experiences with churches, impatience with others' faults, independence, a desire to do everything their way, etc. But because they feel it so strongly, they interpret it as 'God's voice'. Consider the people who say, 'God gave me this song' or 'God gave me this poem' or 'God gave me this book' or 'God gave me the words of this message'. Sometimes we think God has spoken when He has not. Other times we don't think God has spoken when
He has through Scripture, counsel, providential circumstances, including divine appointments, and His still small voice in which He lays people and actions and words on our hearts). I think those who make a habit of saying, 'God told me to...' and finishing the sentences with 'buy this car' or 'post this' or 'ask you to marry me' need to face the fact that just because they feel or want something, even very intensely, does not mean that's what God feels or wants for you. God can speak audibly. Discuss and describe any encounters you may of experienced in hearing from God.
Openly discuss and share your experience.

Chapter Ten

Something old, Something new

'Therefore, if anyone is in Christ, the new creation has come: The old has gone, the new is here'!

- 2 Corinthians 5:17 NIV

Devotion day 1

Love is what binds us together in harmony. It is the foundation of unity, the true key to seeing impossible things. Let's turn our attention one final time to the Garden of Eden. *God created human beings, He created them godlike, reflecting God's nature. He created them able and female. God blessed them; 'Prosper! Reproduce! Fill earth! Take charge! Be responsible for fish in the sea and birds in the air, for every living thing that moves on the face on the earth'*, (Genesis 1:27-28 MSG). This has always been Gods purpose for us. Our past, our fears and the pressures and distortions of our environment come to poison or dilute Gods original plan. Perhaps you have felt too far removed from Eden's assignment to believe it is rightfully yours. Take heart. Every marriage can be re-born and embraced. God not only renovates the past, He makes all things new. He took the trees of Eden, those markers of our downfall and reinvented them. He stretched His son across a tree of death so He could welcome us into His eternity city, home of the tree of life, who's leaves are for the healing of everyone. Nothing that is lost is beyond His power. This includes our marriages. He renews all things. You are allowed to begin again!

Your past is gone! It's cemented in the annals of time and beyond the reach of human efforts. However, there is One who exists outside of time, and He is not bound by its limitations. God will redeem our faults from your past as He rewrites the story of your future. In Gods Kingdom, yesterdays pain does not prevent tomorrow's potential. Each day His mercies are new and His promises await you. He loves, and longs to make impossible things possible for you.

The fruitfulness, effectiveness, and fulfilment God can bring to you individually and to your marriage are beyond anything you can comprehend. Think about your goals, your dreams and your desires you have scripted for your marriage in the past days or weeks. God Himself doesn't want to merely meet that vision. He wants to abundantly exceed it. He longs to deepen your relationship with Him and extend your influence so that your union establishes His Heavenly Kingdom on the earth. He wants to work in and though you in radical ways. Maybe you wouldn't dare of having '*all things new*' again. Maybe you thought you were doomed to never being loved by anyone ever again! Jesus is interested in *your* heart, He is interested in knitting hearts together again.

Once upon a time...

We used to think that if two people had sparks and chemistry when they got married, then the relationship would last. We assumed that modern couples could define love according to their own terms and still have lasting results.

We all experience new seasons from time to time, with some being positive and some negative; some wanted, and some unwanted; some exciting and some terrifying, some old and some new. But regardless of the new that lies before you, how you choose to look at and think about those seasons of newness will determine whether or not you walk through them with peace, hope and joy, or with heartache, anxiety and fear. When we intentionally choose to believe God's *new* is always good, even if you didn't ask for it, want it or understand it, you can step into your new marriage with courage, bravery, a positive attitude and an unsinkable faith. Till death do us part actually means for the rest of your life. And what we're talking about is a daily practice, not a length of time. Forever can be a distraction from what marriage means. The heart of a marriage, the reason that after you and your spouse have fallen madly in love, after you've been through the best and worst, after you've already made your commitment to each other, that then you still go meet the parents and plan the wedding and create the ceremony and gather your loved ones. Why? So that you can declare in a formal way how you will love them. What can you promise today to do for the rest of your life, no matter what arises? What are the aspirations you hold and vow to unfold until you leave this earth? Marriage is not the promise of a dream. When you become confused, lost, or disconnected, what will you vow to do? This is the commitment. How will you love? When things turn out all wrong, what then? Marriage isn't forever. <u>It's for now</u>! Thousands and thousands of nows. Sometimes we choose love. Sometimes we choose anger or blame or resentment. Sometimes we pull away and choose 'I' instead of 'us', But then we remember the vow and we come back. And that's the whole point. Marriage is the vow to return. Letting go of the old frees up your heart to embrace God's *new* for you.

Devotion 1 Questions

Something old, Something new

There's that old rhyme associated with weddings, 'Something old, something new, something borrowed, something blue, and a sixpence in her shoe'. These are the traditional things a Bride is supposed to wear on her wedding day to ensure prosperity and blessings. Letting go of the old, the past and now venturing into a new future, a new hope. Taking on a new name, even looking at a new verse in scripture for encouragement. A new life in God, a new life with your spouse is liberating. Yet, it's also scary because we have to set aside our pre-conceptions. It's all part of entering a new relationship with God as the Bride of Christ. Carefully answer the following with your spouse.

Are you ready to become something new?

_____
_____
_____
_____

Explain the reason behind your willingness to change and to make all things new.

_____
_____
_____
_____
_____

What is stopping you from moving into your new relationship with your spouse or with God? List below anything you feel inside your heart.

_____
_____
_____
_____
_____

What have you learnt from your old past that you won't be bringing into your new future with your spouse. How is God helping you in your season?

_____
_____
_____
_____

Devotion Day 2 Letting go of the old

When there is pain, hurt, grief, anger or sadness in the past, it can develop into emotional baggage, and have an impact on something new in your present or your future. Discuss the following paragraphs with your spouse or in a group setting.

1. **Ask yourself, what actually is causing your pain?** Sometimes we aren't aware of the real issues, we need to get curious. Once we understand what the cause is, we can start to decide on the next step.

2. **Learning to sit with the pain, grief, anger or sadness.** This is an important step towards coping and building your ability to move through the situation. Acknowledge the feeling and accept that it's okay to feel like that. Too often we try and bury it, or brush it away. That only works for a little while and after time it just builds up. Learn to notice the emotion and allow yourself time to breathe slowly through it. Acknowledge the pain and then remind yourself that you will get through this with God.

3. **Identify whether there is something that you can do to resolve the situation.** Often we talk about letting things go but sometimes we need to actually see whether there is something that can be done to change what has happened. This can be a difficult step. It can take time to work through your season and you may want to seek professional help.

4. **Learn to let it go.** Sometimes holding on to the past (something old) can feel comfortable because it's a familiar habit. We think holding on will keep those who have caused the pain to feel punished, when in reality it's us who is being held prisoner. Forgiving means that it doesn't control you or influence your behaviour anymore. Learning to notice your thoughts and challenging those that keep us tied to the past, is going to help you move forward. Isaiah 43:18-19 reads, *'Remember not the former things, nor consider things of old. Behold, I am doing a new thing; now it springs forth, do you not perceive it, I will make a way in the wilderness and rivers in the desert'.*

Whenever I am in a struggle to let go of something, I hold on to this verse. The Lord constantly reminds His people not to dwell on the past. Whatever you are trying to let go of; that past relationship, addiction, or loss, whatever it may be, if you look towards Him and mediate on His Word and promises, He will take care of whatever you are going through and will make a way for you. Jeremiah 29:11 reads; *'For I know the plans I have for you, declares the Lord, plans to prosper you and not harm you, plans to give you hope and a future'.* People do not realise that this was spoken to the people of Israel at one of the lowest points in their history. Our natural tendency is to focus on the 'bad' in a situation. It is part of our wiring and self-preservation to ensure that we protect ourselves from harm. However, God says that if we just look towards Him, we will see the new things He is doing. He wants us to open our eyes to Him. This was very true in my own life when a relationship I was in suddenly came to an end. I spent a long time re-hashing the relationship in my mind, trying to figure out where it had gone wrong, why it didn't get better. Then it finally occurred to me that I was wasting the precious life and time God gave me trying to work out the 'why' for a past event. The truth is the door on that relationship should have been shut from the beginning, it was not a safe space. I was always left wondering where I stood. When I started to focus and read everything the Bible has to say about letting go, my life started to change. God gave me peace; He lifted the sorrow and burden of heartache and I began to see a future, a future of hope and new things happening in my life. Once my time and energy wasn't so consumed by the past, I was now able to operate in the present and look forward to a future. It wasn't the world that gave that gift to me, but a beautiful and graceful gift from God. So, I want to encourage you today, whatever it is you are going through, don't look back to the past, don't dwell on old things, there is nothing there for you. Nothing good comes from looking back. If we dive deep, dwelling on the past can become a form of disobedience, keeping us from doing what God is calling us to right now and the blessed future to come. Train yourself to get into God's Word, and you will also see how it can transform your mind and your entire life. Learning how to unchain yourself from past traumas or regrets is one of the most freeing things you can do for yourself. Not only does it release you from stifling guilt or paralysing fears, but it sets you up to jump into a future that's exciting and fulfilling. It's easier said than done, but letting go of the past and fully stepping into the future can benefit you and your relationships from every direction.

May God's blessing and peace be upon you.

Devotion 2 questions

Letting go of the old

There are many verses in the Bible that talk about letting go and that these could be applied to a wide range of situations in all your life? One of my favourite verses is Isaiah 43:18-19 (ESV), 'Remember not the former things, nor consider things of old. Behold, I am doing a new thing; now it springs forth, do you not perceive it, I will make a way in the wilderness and rivers in the desert'.

So many people from your past know a version of you that doesn't exist anymore. How would you describe who you are today?

_____
_____
_____
_____
_____
_____
_____

Remember, who you were is not who you are, and who you are is not who you will be. You have been redeemed. God will continually be transforming you from glory to glory. For these reasons, and because of His deep love for you, you can leave your past behind.

Briefly describe what your new future looks like. Where do you see God in your future?
_____
_____
_____
_____
_____
_____
_____
_____

Pause and Pray

'LORD BLESS OUR MARRIAGE. THANK YOU THAT I AM A NEW CREATION IN YOU, AND YOU ARE CONTINUING TO REDEEM ALL PARTS OF MY LIFE AND PAST. THANK YOU THAT I NO LONGER NEED TO BE PLAGUED BY GUILT. IN JESUS NAME - AMEN

Devotion Day 3. A Beautiful Cry

'You have collected all my tears in your bottle. You have recorded each one in your book'.

- Psalm 56:8 NLT

I enjoy a good laugh, the kind of laugh where your belly hurts and tears roll down your eyes. You laugh so hard it hurts. Then there's crying. You cry so hard that it makes your mascara run? Or weep until your eyes look red and puffy and your face turns red. We'v all experienced these emotions. Tears are healthy, cleansing, empowering and beautiful. Its ok to cry! I cry with grief and loss. I also cried with tears of joy when our son was born. Joyful tears. Its through every tear that reveals the depths our heart, full of love and wrestling with loss. Tears offer inviting comfort and compassionate care. Crying is not a sign of weakness after all Jesus weeped many times. They can bond our heart to those who also grieve, providing community and the opportunity to comfort someone with the comfort you too received in Christ (2 Corinthians 1:4). Even when nobody sees, I'm assured that

God does. The Psalmist David tells us that God keeps track of our sorrows: *'You have collected all my tears in your bottle. You have recorded each one in your book'* (Psalm 56:8). Like Jesus asked Mary Magdalene beside the empty tomb, our Saviour asks us, *'Why are you weeping'?* (John 20:15 ESV), pausing to listen to the reason for our sorrows. All of our tears are precious to Him. Sometimes grieving people apologise for crying. In the grocery store or doctor's office, they tear up and say, *'I'm sorry, I didn't mean to cry'*. They believe their tears are unwelcome and something to hide. Perhaps you're one of them. I've done this myself, justifying my emotions. Explaining my emotions just to make someone else feel comfortable. Thanks be to God that our sorrows don't make the Great Physician squeamish. They don't make the Prince of Peace restless or discomfited. Instead, Jesus, the man deeply acquainted with grief (Isaiah 53:3), welcomes us to bring our troubles, large and small, to Him. He embraces us with His love, sheltering our wounded hearts like a bird tucks its chicks under its wings (Psalm 17:8). God sees your tears.

It can often feel that in the darkest of our nights God is nowhere to be found. When the storm destroys. When our spouse leaves us. When all we know is loneliness. Does God see our tears? I believe God put Psalm 56 in the Bible for people who feel forgotten in their pain. This Psalm says that every tear David has cried, God has placed in a bottle. It's this intimate imagery that God is near in our hurt. God of all creation is hearing millions of prayers and is aware of every tear that leaves your eyes. Psalm 56:8-11 reads: '*You have kept count of my tossing; put my tears in your bottle. Are they not in your book? This I know, that God is for me. In God, whose word I praise, in the Lord, I shall not be afraid'.*

Let that sink in. There is not a drop of water that has fallen from your eye that God has not seen. Ever. Every burden, painful moment, and anxiety you have faced, God is aware of.

Have you ever thought about the reason we cry? Why would God create a physical act to coincide with our emotional feelings? One reason may be for the social aspect it provides. Think about how difficult pain is when you are alone in it. Tears communicate to others your need for support and love. So in one way, God's designing of tears was actually a design born from His care for us. That tears would symbolise 'I'm hurting' to those near us. Psalm 56 teaches us that God does not simply dismiss our pain. He doesn't acknowledge it and then move on. No, He records them. He keeps record. Personal. Intimate. Caring. This is who our God is.

How beautiful does this make our God? That He is telling us He is aware of *every* tear we cry? He understands, because Jesus felt the burdens we feel. (Hebrews 4:13-16) He felt abandonment from God on the cross. He felt anxiety in the garden when He was sweating blood. He lived day after day with people who doubted who He was, and was constantly misunderstood. He weeped at the loss of his friend, Lazarus. Jesus understands where you are, more than you realise. Ecclesiastes 3:4 reveals that there is *'a time to weep, and a time to laugh; a time to mourn, and a time to dance'*. Jesus expressed the supportive and consoling nature of God toward those distressed by loss when He said, *'Blessed are those who mourn, for they shall be comforted* (Matthew 5:4). Jesus also entered fully into the experience of human sorrow when He wept at the tomb of His friend Lazarus (John 11:35).

Best of all, the Lord in His glorious power will one day *wipe away every tear* (Revelation 21:4). The droplets that once stained our faces will transform into the shining joy of eternal life, and death's terrible curse will be gone.

What beautiful tears those will be!

Devotion 3 Questions
A Beautiful Cry

We often consider crying embarrassing and something to be avoided. 'Big girls don't cry', and a man is considered weak if seen crying. Yet, Jesus Himself wept. Often our problem with crying is that it exposes us, revealing to another our innermost feelings. It forces us to be vulnerable and honest. We don't need to find our identity in having it all together or proving our lives are going great. The gospel has freed us from this. Our worth and righteousness has been perfected in Christ, who promises to use us in our weakness. Our very salvation depends on confessing our weakness and helplessness, so we may receive forgiveness and salvation.

When was the last time you had a big cry? What was the reason?

_____
_____
_____

Where was God in your tears? Who was there to support you? Are you still getting the support you need?

_____
_____
_____
_____
_____

How is your spouse supporting you?

_____
_____
_____
_____
_____

Pause and Pray

'LORD BLESS OUR MARRIAGE. SHOW ME YOU CARE ABOUT ME IN MY SORROW AND PAIN, AND THAT YOU COLLECT EACH TEAR IN YOUR HANDS. REMIND MY ACHING SOUL THAT ONE DAY, YOU PROMISE TO WIPE EVERY TEAR FROM MY EYES. BE NEAR ME.

IN JESUS NAME - AMEN

Devotion Day 4. Known and Loved

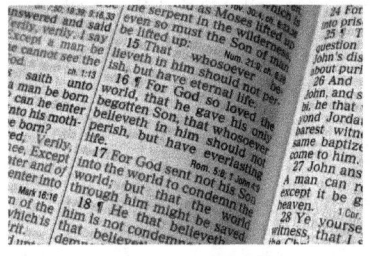

The feelings of being 'known and loved' had been an anthem drumming in the background during some really hard days when I wondered if I'd survive my circumstances. I knew a picture of me wearing this truth would be a good way to declare what I desperately wanted to feel. Instead of feeling known and loved, I felt forgotten and tossed aside. I needed a reminder to turn to God, to open up His Word, and listen to praise songs. When I did those things, I could hear the anthem of God's voice rising above the chaos: *'You are known and so very loved by Me. Trust Me. Follow Me, Don't turn the left or the right. Hold on to Me'*. In my season of grief and healing, God held me when I could barely hang on, and He reminded me what was true when I was tempted to forget. I survived. So will you. What's happened to you hasn't changed who you are. I don't know who in your life has told you that you are anything less than the most glorious creation of the Almighty God. I don't know who has spoken words over you and about you that have stripped you bare and broken your heart. But I do know any statements spoken to you that come against the truth must be called a lie. God's Word is the Truth. His Truth says you are a Holy and dearly loved child of your Heavenly Father. Even if you don't feel known or understood.

Our feelings aren't always an accurate assessment of what's true. Cling to the words of our key verse today: *'And so we know and rely on the love God has for us. God is love. Whoever lives in love lives in God, and God in them'* (1 John 4:16). Release the lies you've believed that make you feel less than who you are, and set your mind and heart on God's Truth.

'Jesus, thank You for the Truth-filled words of Scripture that are always there to remind me who I am. When my insecurities rise up or hurtful comments from others threaten to disrupt the Truth in me, help me believe I am known and loved. Cared for and prayed for. Chosen and cherished. In Jesus' Name, Amen.

Never question God's great love, for it is as unchangeable and part of God as is His holiness. Were it not for the love of God, none of us would ever have a chance in the future life. But God is love! And His love for us is everlasting.

The promises of God's love and forgiveness are as real, as sure, as positive, as human words can make them. But, like describing the ocean, its total beauty cannot be understood until it is actually seen. It is the same with God's love. Until you actually possess true peace with God, no one can describe its wonders to you. God loves you so much, and you are good enough for Him. He showed how much you're worth to Him when Jesus died on the cross and rose from the grave for you. You don't have to earn His love. You don't have to impress anyone. Instead, you can lean into His love and know that, because of Jesus's death and resurrection, you are good enough in His eyes.

What kinds of things make you wonder if God really loves you? Yes, my friend, God knew you before you were ever formed in your mother's womb (Jeremiah 1:5), has numbered the hairs on your head (Luke 12:7), and knows your words completely before they're on your tongue (Psalm 139:4). There is no part of who you are that is hidden from God or is a mystery to Him. So when it seems like the doctors just can't find the problem, or your spouse or friends don't seem to understand you even though they've been right by your side, or all that you've been through feels like more information than you can retain, remember your Creator sees it all. God is aware of every condition you face and each detail about who you are. You can turn to and take refuge in the One who knows your every need, every potential problem, every thought, desire and care. He is familiar with all your ways, and you can trust that you are thoroughly known and loved by Him.

Things people say, expectations you put on yourself, lies you've heard, ways you've been mistreated, etc.? The enemy always wants us to doubt God's love for us. Because of Jesus' death and resurrection, we can be confident that *'nothing in all creation will ever be able to separate us from the love of God that is revealed in Christ Jesus our Lord'* (Romans 8:39).

God loves you. Yes! Unconditional. Undeniable. Unlimited. You are His precious beloved child, made in the image of your Creator. Created for love to be loved and to love. And there is more. God is love. Pure love poured out on you like a rushing waterfall after a torrential rainfall, cool and comforting in the heat of the day or the heat of the moment. No matter your situation, single, married, divorced, widow, widower, orphan, successful, failure, working, out of work, rich, poor, good or bad, you are uniquely and passionately loved. Loved by the gentle, forgiving touch of your heavenly Father. Loved by the brotherly friendship and romantic passion of Jesus Christ, and loved by the comfort, compassion and guidance of the Holy Spirit. Yes, Jesus loves you.

Devotion 4 Questions
Known and Loved

Read the following verses as a couple or in a group setting. Allow God to speak to you through His Word. Be open to healing and prayer.

You are wonderfully made (Psalm 139:14)

You are a treasure (1 Peter 2:9)

You are beautiful (1 Peter 3:4)

You are fully known by Him and lavishly loved by Him (Psalm 139:1-4)

You are chosen (Ephesians 1:11)

You are special (Ephesians 2:10)

You are full of purpose (Romans 8:28)

How well do you receive the love of the community and from fellow followers of Jesus?

_____
_____
_____
_____
_____
_____

Have you ever asked God to show you a sign of His love? What was the response?

_____
_____
_____
_____
_____
_____

Pause and Pray

'LORD BLESS OUR MARRIAGE. BLESS US WITH LOVE, THAT WE MAY LOVE AS YOU LOVE! .

IN JESUS NAME - AMEN

Devotion Day 5. A United Marriage

Creating a marriage that embodies a true partnership takes dedication and intentionality. To neglect the effort required can be disastrous. The enemy of *best* can be as subtle as compromising for what seems *good*. As my husband and I have supported each other in our own marriage and encouraged other couples over the years, we've identified three characteristics of united marriages, each of which is anchored by this verse: *'And let us **consider** how we may **spur one another on** toward **love and good deeds**'* (Hebrews 10:24, emphases added). The Greek word translated as *'consider'* in Hebrews 10:24 is *katanoeo*. It means to pay attention, notice or observe. To consider is no small thing; it requires devoted time, focus and care. To *'spur on'* means to engage, encourage, plan and remove obstacles. *'Love and good deeds'*, then, become the execution of a harmonious and shared vision.

Spouses in a united marriage consider each other's gifts. We ask questions and imagine possibilities beyond what our spouse might consider for themselves. Partnership requires reciprocity, which means each spouse is willing to sacrifice their own priorities to benefit their spouse. United couples are unselfish and passionate in their desire to cultivate each other's gifts.

Spouses in a united marriage activate and engage by spurring each other on. None of us does well alone. When self-doubt kicks in and we ask ourselves, *'Do I have what it takes'?* our spouse can respond with love and affirmation, recognising the ways we make an impact. In conversations with friends, a 'spurring' spouse brags about our latest project or venture and celebrates our wins.**Spouses in a united marriage live a shared vision of love and good deeds.** Discerning God's bigger vision for our marriage requires time, investigation and prayer. Spouses can ask, 'What love and good deeds has God set out for us to accomplish together? If we could do anything together to make the world a better place, what would it be'? We contemplate how God may want to use us as a couple, even as a family, to bring His healing and peace to those who need it most. What Does Healthy Unity in Marriage Look Like? The healthiest marriages I've seen are those in which both parties maintain separate identities and purposes as they unite under the shared purpose of fulfilling the dominion rule of God in and through their partnership. This understanding of unity offers each person in the marriage the opportunity to experience the maximum freedom that God intended for His creation to enjoy. Within the boundaries of the marriage relationship, both the husband and wife are to fully pursue their calling under God utilising their gifts to advance the potential of the other in an atmosphere of mutual trust and respect, so long as Biblical priorities of the unity of the family are not being compromised.

Maintaining your personal space, preferences, and identity just might be the biggest challenge in your marriage. It's possible that you may not even realise it. When so much of life converges with another human being, it's easy to lose who you are and to let your own candle blow out. But the greatest gift you can give your unity is to maintain your individual uniqueness. Because when two strong and sure people come together under the Lord, utilising their gifts, minds, and spirits according to His plan, a greater kingdom impact will occur. God didn't create marriage for us all to fail. He loves your marriage, and He loves you. God restores. God repurposes. God makes all things new. Making Jesus LORD over your marriage is choosing love and forgiveness in the good, the bad, and the ugly. Take a spiritual stand today. Submit yourself to

God's plan. Have a look at the last chapter in the book Cinderella. The last verse reads: '...and they lived happily ever after'. Turn to the last chapter in the book of Sleeping Beauty. The last verse reads: '...and they lived happily ever after'. And then, if you turn to the last chapter in the book Snow White, the last verse reads: '...and they lived happily ever after'. We all long for the fairy-tale ending. We're not asking much, we just want to be able to live 'happily ever after'. Most people associate happiness with pleasure. God wants you to be happy, and the only way is by taking notice of his Son Jesus Christ who said, *'I have come in order that you might have life, and life in its fullest'*. Resist the urge to quit, complain, and become numb today, in Jesus' name. Ask God for help. Pray about everything! Surrender your will to His. Take authority over your marriage in Jesus' name, and use it. Take the cotton buds of complaining out of your ears and listen to what the Holy Spirit is speaking to you today. The Holy Spirit is cheering your marriage on, convicting you of sin, guiding you in truth, and giving you power to live for Jesus. Choosing to hear and obey today will lead to beautiful fruit in your already blessed marriage.

Devotion 5 Questions

A United Marriage

A united marriage consists of 5 practical steps; for example, prayer, collecting inspiration, dating, setting goals and dreams, and determination to reach them. Your marriage will cover many seasons in life. With these goals in mind, answer the following questions together. 'What will our marriage look like when we are...

Married with children? Will you do it alone? Or get family members involved to help raise your children?

_____
_____
_____
_____

Raising young children? Traditional or modern views?

_____
_____
_____
_____

Parenting pre-teens/teenagers? Are you prepared to discuss topics such as puberty, sex and how babies are made? The warnings signs of addictions and dating? Who will set the ground rules in your marriage?

_____
_____
_____
_____

Empty nesters? Your children have left home. Who will look after you in your old age?

_____
_____
_____
_____

Enjoying your grandchildren? Taking turns sharing the grandchildren with in-laws on special occasions?

_____
_____
_____
_____
_____
_____

Knowing God makes things new, if you are single, dating, engaged, married or re-marrying, how can you internally position yourself for the marriage you desire in the future? Write the steps you need to take.

_____
_____
_____
_____
_____

You've set goals for finances, parenting, careers and holidays. These are big picture visions for you both. They will need to be supported by your standards, values, choices, and habits in the day-to day.

Think about the following questions. Openly discuss them as a couple or a group setting.

- How and when will you handle your monthly budget?

- What type of holidays will you take? How will you plan them?

- What kind of activities, hobbies and entertainment will you enjoy together?

- How will you continue to date your spouse?
- How will you resolve differences with your spouse?
- How will you invest in your spiritual well-being?
- How will you raise your children in the knowledge of God?
- How will you discipline your children?
- How will support each others careers and goals?
- How will you celebrate special occasions?

Every relationship is shaped by countless daily interactions, how you communicate, support each other, and work through challenges together. Over time, these patterns reveal the true foundation of your marriage.

Remember a marriage is knitted together with friendship, commitment and God's Covenant everything else is life!

From the Author

Thank you for taking the time to invest in what God created. Your marriage! I write to express my deepest gratitude for your unwavering support and heartfelt enthusiasm throughout this incredible journey of marriage. There is nothing more empowering and inspiring than knowing that my words have touched your hearts, re-kindled your imaginations, and provided respite from the trials of everyday life. Your loyalty and dedication are deeply appreciated. I hope you have enjoyed working through this Devotional Workbook and have been open to further growth and development within your marriage.

I hope through studying the topics you have been challenged, healed, and enriched in your knowledge.

Your encouragement has been amazing through countless hours of creating both *'Whispers of Marriage from EDEN'* and the *'Devotional Workbook'*. I have unpacked many everyday topics. Your uplifting messages, heartfelt reviews, and unwavering support are the fuel that keeps me passionately motivated to feed relationships with Gods unconditional love. Thank you for sharing with me your breathtaking moments, and ultimately, your happily ever afters.

Each time you recommend my book to friends and family, it fills me with an immense sense of pride and fulfilment. The emails I receive detailing how my book have shaped your lives is a constant reminder of why I pour so much of myself into each written word, and why I desire to see people live a marriage filled with hope and healing, not hurt and pain.

It is for readers like you that I devote endless nights crafting each chapter, that transports you straight into the living word of Gods truth for love.

From the bottom of my heart, thank you for embracing the moments shared between each testimony as well as the journey we embarked upon through out those stories.

I promise to continue striving to equip future generations with valuable tools, knowledge, experience as well as Biblical applications into the very essence of what can become their happily ever after.

With heartfelt appreciation

Rachelle M Smith

End Notes

- English *biologist* David Attenborough, https://www.google.com/url?sa=t&source=web&rct=j&opi=89978449&url=https://www.discoverwildlife.com/people/david-attenborough-facts&ved=2ahUKEwihne-yhbSOAxWiamwGHbOqIdwQFnoECGwQAQ&usg=AOvVaw1SFe-Foj7AlUCZEBM1NVK_

- Covey, R, Steven; Quote - *'To begin with the end in mind means to start with a clear understanding of your destination. It means to know where you're going so that you better understand where you are now and so that the steps you take are always in the right direction'.*

- Eliezer Gonzalez - © 2018-2021, Good News Unlimited Ltd, *'Unlimited: Jesus Wants To Focus on Our Hearts'*, Sept 1, 2021.

- Chip Ingram, *Living one the Edge.*

ORDER DETAILS

Whispers of Marriage from EDEN - Paperback

DEVOTIONAL WORKBOOK - Paperback

Whispers of Marriage from EDEN - Amazon Kindle

 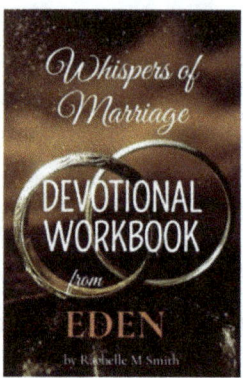 

Book orders can be made through Lulu Bookstore and ebook Kindle using the following websites:

  amazon kindle

 SJ & RM Publishing
https://www.whispersofmarriagefromeden.com

 https://www.facebook.com/rachelle.smith.986282

If you wish to write a recommendation. Please write a short review on the Amazon Kindle App. Your written expression is greatly appreciated. Reviews from readers like you, make a difference to encouraging couples who need it most.